For Angela

Hauntingly yours,
Kathryn T. Windham
and
JEFFREY

January 20, 1979

⑬
Thirteen Georgia Ghosts
And Jeffrey

FIRST PRINTING — 1973
SECOND PRINTING — 1974
THIRD PRINTING — 1977

🄵 Thirteen Georgia Ghosts And Jeffrey

by

Kathryn Tucker Windham

Illustrations and Jacket
by
Frances Lanier

The Strode Publishers
Huntsville, Alabama

Printed in United States of America
Library of Congress Catalogue Number: 73-87004
Standard Book Number: 87397-041-1

LAYOUT AND DESIGN BY BECKY SHARPE

Contents

v

"Jeffrey The Ghost" Series

13 Alabama Ghosts And Jeffrey
by Kathryn Tucker Windham
Margaret Gillis Figh

Jeffrey Introduces 13 More Southern Ghosts
by Kathryn Tucker Windham

13 Georgia Ghosts And Jeffrey
by Kathryn Tucker Windham

All photographs in this book were taken by Kathryn Windham at the actual scene of each story. Anyone wishing to visit the ghostly haunts can——at his own risk.

Foreword

Jeffrey is the ghost who lives in the Windham home in Selma, Alabama.

He is a friendly poltergeist who clumps around the house, frightens the cat (an aged feline known as Hornblower), and delights in creating confusion. His pranks are mischievous rather than wicked, and his antics provide the Windhams and their friends with unusual and rather spirited pleasure.

Jeffrey's presence in her home stirred Kathryn Windham's latent interest in the subject of ghosts, and she began a collection of authentic ghost stories from throughout the South.

In collaboration with Margaret Gillis Figh, folklore authority on the Huntingdon College (Montgomery, Alabama) faculty, she wrote *13 Alabama Ghosts and Jeffrey.* This book was followed by *Jeffrey Introduces 13 More Southern Ghosts,* a sampling of strange tales from seven southern states.

Now, still prodded by Jeffrey, Kathryn Windham has selected thirteen of Georgia's grandest ghosts for inclusion in this latest volume of true tales of the supernatural.

Preface

Kathryn Windham is a professional compiler of ghost stories, and in *13 Georgia Ghosts And Jeffrey* she has drawn from the best of Georgia's wealth of ghostlore. Most of these specters are famous, known throughout the South; a few are familiar only in their own locality. All of them have an authentic historical background.

Ghost stories have a very real place in the folklore and the history of a state or a nation. After all, who should be better able to tell of happenings long past than the ghosts of those who had a part in them?

Kathryn Windham (with the aid of Jeffrey) has a talent for making ghost stories interesting to all ages—from third graders to doctors of philosophy—and making history come alive in the process. Her talent was never better than in *13 Georgia Ghosts And Jeffrey*.

Miss Bessie Lewis
Historical Consultant
Georgia Historical Commission

The Ghost Collie At Scataway

They tell strange tales up in the mountains of north Georgia, up around Owl Town and Shake Rag and Lower Tater Ridge, tales of monsters and witches and boogers and other embodiments of evil, but it is the story of the white collie, a gentle and pathetic dog, that is told most often at Scataway.

Some people now living in the Scataway community that sprawls along the mountain valley have seen the ghost collie and can give personal testimony of these encounters. Other stories of the phantom dog begin, "My grandpa used to tell me—," or, "Mama's oldest sister, Aunt Vonnie, said she—." The accounts, though they may vary in detail, all relate the story of a white collie that used to return from the dead to search for his owner in Scataway.

Perhaps no one tells the story of the sorrowing animal better than does Hugh Oliver. Hugh Oliver left his rugged, unspoiled hills to find adventure in far countries, and he has now returned to claim fulfillment at a place called Bald Mountain Park.

"I saw the ghost dog," Hugh Oliver says, "and I patted

11

him. And he licked my hand. It's been more than forty years ago, but I can still remember how his fur felt, and I can still feel his tongue licking my hand."

Hugh was about eight years old when it happened, and he was visiting his older sister at Scataway. The sister was named Blon, Miss Blon Oliver, and she was the teacher at the one-room Scataway school.

School zones were vague, and enforcement of attendance laws was lax in those days, so sometimes when Miss Blon came home for the weekend, Hugh would go back to Scataway with her and attend school there for a week or two.

Miss Blon boarded with Mr. and Mrs. Silas Deaton, an elderly couple who lived about a quarter of a mile from the frame schoolhouse. Nearly everybody in Scataway, even people not kin to them, called the couple Grandma and Grandpa Deaton, sort of titles of affection and respect.

The Deatons' house was right close to the main road that came through the gap and ran through the valley. It was not a big house, but it was comfortable and Miss Blon liked boarding there. She had a small bedroom that opened off the front room, the main room in the house. Her furniture was plain: a feather bed, a straight chair and a table (both handmade) to hold her books, a washstand with a bowl and pitcher. The floor was bare, its wide boards worn smooth by many feet and many scrubbings. The room's only decorations were an oval picture of a nameless Deaton ancestor in a flat frame, a cross-stitched sampler with colored X's spelling out "The Lord Is My Shepherd," and a calendar with a picture of a lighthouse on it. Miss Blon had promised to save the picture for Hugh when the year ended.

Grandma and Grandpa Deaton liked to have Hugh come to visit them. When she knew he was coming, Grandma Deaton would make teacakes and have them tied in a clean flour sack in the corner of the kitchen safe. Hugh knew where to find

12

Hugh Oliver re-visits the school where his sister taught.

them.

Grandpa Deaton would show Hugh how to whittle an airplane, complete with a propeller that really twirled, though neither of them had ever seen an airplane close up. Grandpa Deaton also carved tiny baskets out of peach seeds, and they made whang-doodles and tops, too. Once Grandpa Deaton whittled out a wooden chain with thirteen links, but he would not give it to Hugh until the boy could name the thirteen colonies. It was a history lesson Hugh never forgot.

Miss Blon enjoyed Hugh's visits, too. "Hugh's a help to me," she would tell their parents when Hugh asked permission to go over to Scataway with her.

Hugh did try to help. He carried Miss Blon's books and their lunch pail when they walked to school in the early mornings. In the wintertime he took out the ashes and helped build a fire in the iron stove that heated the schoolroom. After he had warmed his hands and his feet, Hugh would take the water bucket from the shelf near the window and go to the well to get fresh drinking water for the day.

He never volunteered to help Miss Blon with the sweeping, but occasionally after school, after all the other children had left, Hugh would volunteer to wash the blackboard. He did not want any of the boys to see him doing what he considered to be girls' work.

Though Hugh Oliver has many tales to tell of his childhood visits to Scataway, his strangest story is of the night the ghost collie came.

It had been a night like many other nights. They had eaten supper in the kitchen close to the wood range, and after supper Hugh had brought in an armload of logs for the big fireplace in the front room. He had sat on a braided rug, one Grandma Deaton had made, in front of the fire and had listened to Grandpa Deaton tell tales of his boyhood. Miss Blon was grading papers, and Grandma Deaton was picking

14

out hickory nuts.

Hugh was sleepy. He had gotten up early to go to school with his sister, and he had played many games of whoopy-hide at recess, at noontime and after school. Now the warmth of the fire and the soothing rhythm of Grandpa Deaton's voice made him drowsy.

He was glad when Miss Blon put her schoolwork away and said, "Well, Hugh, it's time we went to bed." Hugh undressed quickly and stood warming by the fire while Grandpa Deaton read a chapter from the Bible. Then he gave the adults a good-night hug and ran to bed.

The stack of quilts—bear paw, Jacob's ladder, star, all pieced by Grandma Deaton—felt good. He was nearly asleep when Miss Blon reached beneath the covers and wrapped his feet in a wool sweater she had warmed by the fire. He was asleep when Miss Blon made sure the window was tightly closed, buttoned the door, and crawled into bed beside him.

The next thing Hugh knew he was wide awake. It was near dawn but sunrise was still a promise, and the room held the greyness of fading night. At first Hugh could not decide what had waked him. Miss Blon was still asleep, and there was no sound of Grandma or Grandpa Deaton stirring. Some noise had aroused him though, some unusual noise. Hugh lay still and listened.

He heard it again, the noise that had called him from sleep, quite distinctly this time: he heard the scratchy padding of a dog's feet across the bare floor. Then he heard panting, the way a dog does when he has run a long way.

Hugh looked over the edge of the bed, and there sitting on his haunches and looking right at him was a dog, a big white collie. The boy instinctively reached out to pat the dog, to run his fingers through his fur. The dog licked Hugh's hand.

Suddenly Hugh felt uneasy. Something was wrong. Grandma and Grandpa Deaton did not have a dog; in all his

15

visits to Scataway he had never seen a dog at their home. And how had the animal gotten into the room? The window was still closed, the door was buttoned.

Hugh was frightened. "Blon! Blon!" he called as he shook his sister's shoulder. "Blon!"

"What is it, Hugh? What's wrong?" Blon asked sleepily. Then, seeing the look on his face, she said,

"You saw the dog, didn't you? The white collie."

"Yes—but how did you know?" Hugh replied. "How could you know?"

"He comes often, and—"

"He's here now," Hugh interrupted, "right by the bed."

But when he looked, the dog was gone.

The window was still closed, the door still buttoned. There had been no sound, no clicking of claws on the bare floor, but the white collie was gone.

"Don't be frightened," Miss Blon said, gathering Hugh in her arms. "It's all right. I can't explain it. All I know is that he's a ghost dog that comes here every now and then. Grandpa Deaton says he's looking for somebody. He's friendly but kind of sad. Don't be upset—it's all right," she said again.

They could hear Grandpa Deaton moving around then, could hear the clatter of the metal eyes as he started a fire in the kitchen stove and could hear him stirring up the coals and adding kindling to coax a blaze in the front room fireplace.

Hugh wondered if Grandpa Deaton had seen the dog, too.

"Come on—let's get dressed," Miss Blon urged. "You can go dress in the front room by the fire."

"He licked my hand. That dog licked my hand right here," Hugh said, holding out his hand to his sister.

Miss Blon held Hugh's hand and looked first at the spot he showed her and then deep into his eyes. "Here," she said, handing him a wet washrag, "Wash your face and hands for

16

breakfast."

Hugh was not hungry. He sat at the table, but he could not eat breakfast. He could not even drink the hot chocolate Grandma Deaton had fixed for him.

"What's wrong, boy? You sick?" Grandpa Deaton asked.

"He saw the dog, the white collie," Miss Blon explained. "He saw the dog, and it upset him."

"Come here, boy," Grandpa Deaton said. He took Hugh's hand and led him into the front room. Then he sat in front of the fire and held Hugh on his knees while he told the story of the white collie.

"A long time ago, back when there weren't many people or many houses in this valley, a man and his wife lived right here in this house. Nobody seems to know for sure what their names were. Maybe they were named Henson. That's a good name.

"Travelers coming through the valley would often stop here to spend the night. Mrs. Henson would cook them a good supper, and Mr. Henson would help see after their horse or their mule. Some folks didn't have a horse or a mule—they'd come walking in with a pack of stuff on their back.

"Sometimes the travelers would sleep in the room where Miss Blon sleeps now. If it was winter and cold or if there were a good many travelers here the same night, they might sleep here on the floor in front of the fire.

"Well, one time a man stopped here—he'd been before, maybe half a dozen times—and he told Mrs. Henson, 'I've brought you a surprise.' And he reached inside his coat and he brought out the cutest little fuzzy puppy you ever did see. Solid white. Just a ball of white fur.

"The puppy looked so much like a snowball, that's what they started to name it, but Mrs. Henson said that was too common a name. She wanted her dog to have a special name,

17

not like every other white dog was named, so she named him Frost. Frost can be mighty white and thick too, you know.

"Frost kinda got to be a pet with everybody. He grew to be a big, friendly dog, and he liked just about everybody, but it seemed like he knew he was Mrs. Henson's dog, and he really loved that woman. He'd follow her around, and he'd lie down close to her when she was working in the kitchen—not get in the way, you know, just be close.

"Folks who stopped often at the Henson's house got real fond of Frost, and some of them even gave him presents. The cobbler made Frost a leather collar, all hand-tooled and decorated, while he was in the community mending shoes, and a tinker made Frost a big tin bowl with his name around the rim. Hunters were all the time bringing Frost big bones to gnaw on.

"Well, late one winter afternoon this man came riding up and asked if he could spend the night. Mr. Henson went to the door when the man knocked. He didn't like the fellow's looks and would have turned him away, but the weather was uncommonly cold and cloudy and looking like snow, and Mr. Henson hated to send anybody out in a mountain storm.

"So he told the man he could come on in and spend the night—if he didn't mind sleeping in front of the fire. You see, Mr. Henson knew Mrs. Henson wasn't going to let anybody dirty as that stranger sleep in her good bed.

"Frost didn't like the stranger at all. Soon as the man walked into the front room, Frost commenced to growl real low and to move up close to Mrs. Henson. Mrs. Henson tried to calm the dog, but it was plain that Frost didn't want the man in the house.

"Well, Frost got so riled up that Mr. Henson finally shut him up in the bedroom so Mrs. Henson could fix supper, but Frost scratched on the door and barked and cut up so bad they had to let him out.

18

"Mrs. Henson held Frost by the collar and kept saying she was sorry for the way the dog was acting and telling the man that Frost never had bitten anybody, but you could tell that the man didn't like Frost any better than Frost liked him. He was scared of Frost, too.

"Now nobody knows exactly what happened later on that night.

"Next afternoon, somebody passing the house stopped to speak to the Hensons. The visitor called a couple of times but nobody answered, and he whistled for Frost, but Frost didn't come.

"The man felt like something was wrong, so he went to get some help. Some men working down the road came with him and broke open the door, and they found Mr. and Mrs. Henson dead. Murdered. Frost was dead, too. He was lying right at Mrs. Henson, like he might have been trying to protect her.

"Folks figured that the stranger, whoever he was, must have thought the Hensons had some money hid at their house, and he aimed to rob them. It was a bad thing. Real bad.

"The house stayed empty a long time after that. Nobody wanted to live in it. Then finally some new people moved in, folks who didn't know anything about what had happened to the Hensons.

"They'd been living there a good while when the man asked somebody after preaching one Sunday if he knew anything about a white collie. Said they kept seeing the dog around the place. Said the dog would just come from nowhere—just come—and then he'd disappear the same way. Said the dog never would eat anything, that he'd just walk through the house like he was looking for somebody he knew and missed.

"The way he described the dog, the collar and all, folks at church knew it was Frost. Couldn't have been any other dog.

"We, Grandma and I, been living here a long time now, and ever since we've been here, we've been seeing that dog, Frost. Sometimes we'll be sitting before the fire here in the front room, and we'll look and there'll be a big white dog sitting on his haunches right there between us. He'll sit there and look at the fire. Won't lie down, just sit there. Then he'll walk around like he's hoping to find somebody. Then he'll go away.

"So that's the dog you saw in Miss Blon's room this morning, that's the ghost collie. He's still looking for his mistress."

"I can still remember how his fur felt when I petted him. And I can still feel his tongue licking my hand," Hugh Oliver says.

Could these be the tracks of the ghost collie?

The Eternal Dinner Party

"Father, what will be your wedding gift to me? Please tell me!" Mary Mulryne teased.

John Mulryne looked at his daughter and smiled. "It is a secret," he said. "I told you it was to be a secret, and it will remain a secret until I am ready to divulge it to you."

"O, Father!" Mary pouted. "How can you be so cruel? Give me a hint—please! Is it big? What color is it? Are there many like it in the shops in Charleston? Please give me a hint!"

"You could never guess what it is. Never," her father replied. He was very pleased with the wedding gift he had planned for his daughter. He was pleased, too, with her choice of a husband, for the marriage of Mary Mulryne to Josiah Tattnall would unite two of the colonies' most prominent families.

The Mulrynes and the Tattnalls had been friends in Charleston, and when Colonel Mulryne moved his family to Savannah in the late 1750s young Josiah Tattnall came soon afterwards to seek Mary's hand in marriage.

Before the couple's wedding in 1760 Colonel Mulryne had

completed his great house on the outskirts of Savannah. Built of brick imported from England (Colonel Mulryne was a very wealthy man), the house sat on a plateau overlooking the Wilmington River. Terraced gardens extended from the front of the house down to the water where a boat landing jutted into the stream.

He called his home Bonaventure.

Much of the planting of the grounds had been completed, but Colonel Mulryne planned the most spectacular landscaping feat in all of Georgia for his daughter's wedding gift. On the acres surrounding his home Colonel Mulryne supervised the planting of hundreds of live oak trees in the pattern of an M entwined with a T.

"This," he told his daughter, "is your gift: oaks planted to form the initials of Mulryne and Tattnall to celebrate the joining together of these two families. The trees will grow more beautiful with the years—and so will your marriage."

Mary was charmed by the originality of the gift, and she was touched by her father's display of pride and sentiment.

"O, Father, it's wonderful!" she exclaimed. "And you were right—I would never have been able to guess a gift as perfect as my trees."

There were other gifts, too, including the manor house itself, but it was the trees that Mary loved. They flourished in the coastal air, and as they grew and their patterned planting became more distinct, Mary delighted in strolling about the grounds with her guests and pointing out the entwined M and T formed by the trees.

She walked beneath the oaks with her young sons John and Josiah, Jr., and she told them the story of the plantings.

"I hope you will walk in the shade of these trees—my wedding trees—when you are old, old men," she would tell her sons, and they would laugh at the foolishness of ever growing old as children always laugh at make believe and pretend.

Then there came a time when it seemed that strangers would own Bonaventure and would walk beneath the oaks, strangers to whom the entwined initials would mean nothing. The Revolution came, and the Mulrynes and the Tattnalls were Tories, loyal to King George III and his colonial government.

It was to Bonaventure that the Royal Governor of Georgia, James Wright, fled for sanctuary when he escaped from the Patriots assigned to guard him. Governor Wright was arrested at his Savannah home on January 18, 1776, and upon his promise that he would not communicate with the British ships then lying just outside the harbor he was permitted to remain at his residence. Perhaps as the sentiment against the King and as intolerance for Loyalists increased, Governor Wright began to fear for his safety. In any event he broke his pledge, slipped from his home, and made his way to Bonaventure about a month after his arrest.

Colonel Mulryne had aided in the governor's escape, and together the two old friends got into a small boat at the landing at Bonaventure and were rowed out to the British ship *Scarborough*. The captain of the vessel received Governor Wright and Colonel Mulryne on board at 3:00 o'clock in the morning on February 12.

Colonel Mulryne, after he left Georgia, went to Nassau in the Bahamas where he later died. The governor went into exile in Nova Scotia, waiting there for three and one-half years until the British regained control of Savannah and he was summoned to head the civil government there.

Josiah Tattnall's avowed loyalty to the King and his open denounciation of the colonies' revolt against England made him a marked man among the revolutionaries in Georgia. Although he had not taken up arms on the side of the British, his Patriot neighbors knew where his sympathies lay, and

25

they distrusted and reviled him.

The feeling against the Tory Tattnalls grew so rapidly and became so bitter that Josiah Tattnall felt it wise to make speedy arrangements to take his family to England for safety. He was engaged in preparing for their departure, sorting papers and gathering up documents in his study, when his twelve-year-old son, Josiah Tattnall, Jr., entered the book-lined room and said firmly,

"Father, I am not going to England. Georgia is my home. I will stay here and join the Patriots and fight for freedom. I love Georgia, and I belong here."

Tattnall was so astounded at this rebellious outburst from his son that he dropped the sheaf of papers he was holding and reached out to grab him, thinking to shake some sense into his head. Then he stopped himself. After all, he reasoned, the child was too young to realize what he was saying. He had obviously been listening to too much talk by the Liberty Boys and had been taken in by their distorted notions of freedom.

So he did not touch the boy though he did speak harshly to him.

"There will be no talk of rebellion against our King in this house!" he declared. "You will go to your room and remain there—I will send a servant to lock your door—until we leave tonight. You will go to England with us, and you will be a loyal subject of King George. Now go to your room!"

After he had made sure that Josiah, Jr., was locked securely in his room (there was no time to chase a runaway boy across the countryside), Tattnall tried to return to the work in his study. However, he found he could not concentrate. The exchange with his son had upset him, and he wondered how he could have been so totally unaware of where young Josiah's sympathies lay. He kept hearing Josiah say, "I love Georgia," and he wondered about the depth of that love.

"He'll get over this foolish display of sympathy for the Revolution," Tattnall told himself. "By the time we sail tonight he will be excited, as any child would be, over our trip to England. He'll be all right."

But when night came, Josiah, even though he had been confined to his room all day to "consider the error of his ways," was still rebellious and defiant.

"I will not leave Georgia!" he shouted as soon as his father unlocked his door. His father had to grab him before the boy went streaking from the house.

So Josiah Tattnall, Jr., was carried bodily to the river landing and placed in a boat that took his family and their possessions out to where the England-bound ship waited.

Once on board ship Josiah slipped away from the servant assigned to watch him, dived overboard, and began swimming toward shore. Only prompt action by a sailor who dived into the water after him saved the child from drowning—or from making good his escape to Georgia and the fight for freedom there.

After his rescue, Josiah was locked in his cabin until the ship was well out to sea.

These displays of headstrong stubbornness angered Tattnall, but he tried to assure himself that his son would outgrow such childishness. But Josiah never outgrew his love for his native country, and nothing he saw in England was ever as beautiful to him as his memories of Bonaventure and the oaks and the river and the marshes back in Georgia. He read with interest the news dispatches telling of the progress of the war in America, and when those dispatches reported a victory for Washington's troops, he gloated. He kept his feelings to himself though for he knew of no one in England who shared his devotion to the Patriots' cause.

The Tattnalls had lived in England nearly six years when

27

Josiah, who was then a student at Eton, approached his father and said,

"Father, I am old enough to make my own decisions now. I want to return to Georgia and fight with the Patriots. I am asking for your permission to do this."

Tattnall refused to give his permission (there was a bitter scene, and Tattnall almost gave his son the shaking he had withheld years before), so Josiah Tattnall, Jr., left England without it. Within a few weeks Josiah had arrived in Georgia and had joined the forces of General Nathaniel Greene.

When the Tattnalls left Georgia, Bonaventure had been confiscated by the Patriots, but when an heir to the property returned from England to aid in their fight for independence, the Patriots returned part of the family estate, including his birthplace, to Josiah Tattnall, Jr.

It was to Bonaventure that Josiah, after the Revolution, brought his bride. He told her the romantic story of the planting of the oaks, and, as he walked beneath them with his bride, he marveled at how large the trees had grown during the years he had been away.

Josiah was a leader in organizing the government of the new state of Georgia, and he was entrusted with positions of authority. He reached the rank of brigadier general of the First Brigade of the Georgia Militia, was elected to the Georgia Legislature, served in Congress, and was for one year before his death governor of Georgia.

He and his wife were also prominent in the social life of Savannah—in much of Georgia, really—and they often entertained with parties and balls and banquets. Bonaventure provided the perfect setting for these events.

Party guests from neighboring plantations—Wormsloe, Greenwich, Vernonburg, and others—often came by boat, and the distinctive chant of their oarsmen announced the approach of each contingent. Inland guests arrived by

The oak trees are still at Bonaventure, their gnarled limbs softened by the streamers of moss.

carriage and were met by grooms who cared for their horses at the Tattnall stables while the party was in progress. By whatever route they came, visitors approached the house along curved walkways beneath the branches of the live oak trees.

The Tattnalls were hosting one of their biggest parties of the holiday season when tragedy struck Bonaventure.

The invitations (each one hand-lettered and decorated with tiny watercolors of native flowers) to the affair, a dinner party set for just before Thanksgiving, had been personally delivered, and for days the cooks, under Mrs. Tattnall's supervision, had been planning and preparing the menu. There would be the usual hams and turkeys, of course, supplemented by wild duck with orange sauce, oyster casseroles, corn souffle, candied sweet potatoes, and tiny white onions cooked in a creamy sauce that only Mrs. Tattnall knew how to prepare. In addition to imported champagne, wines, and brandies there would be a clear, sweet scuppernong wine made from the grapes from their own long arbor, and there would be rich, airy syllabub served in slender glasses.

The downstairs rooms were decorated with greenery from the plantation—smilax, holly, and magnolia leaves—and lighted lanterns were hung from trees along the front walk.

Although it was late November, the night was not chilly. Winter arrived late that year, and the weather remained unusually balmy until almost Christmastime.

There was really no need for a fire, but at Mrs. Tattnall's urging Tattnall lighted the logs in the wide fireplaces in the downstairs parlors. The firelight, Mrs. Tattnall said, was romantic and decorative and added a festive touch which somehow made the entire house seem more hospitable and inviting.

Each group of guests who arrived commented,

30

"Bonaventure never looked lovelier," and Mr. and Mrs. Tattnall smiled with each new underlining of the awareness of the beauty of their home.

Mrs. Tattnall, who was somewhat inclined to get a bit upset or flustered when large numbers of guests came for a formal meal, was delighted with the success of the party. Everything was going splendidly, and even the new serving girl, about whom she had been apprehensive, was performing her duties admirably. Mrs. Tattnall found it easy to smile and relax and enjoy her guests.

The diners had been seated at the banquet table and were beginning their first course when the butler walked swiftly into the dining room and whispered something to Mr. Tattnall. The host asked to be excused and followed the butler into the kitchen.

Mrs. Tattnall knew that something most extraordinary had occurred to take her husband away from his guests. The guests, too, were aware that something was amiss, but, being polite, they continued the meal.

In a very few minutes, Mr. Tattnall returned to the dining room and said calmly,

"Ladies and gentlemen, I must apologize to you. We will have a slight interruption in our dinner.

"Please rise and follow me out into the garden. My servants will bring the table and chairs outside, and we will continue our dinner there.

"Bonaventure is on fire and will soon be destroyed by flames," he added. Neither his voice nor his expression changed. He spoke as casually as though he were inviting friends to shelter from a sudden shower.

He looked straight at his wife, signaling her to remain calm, and the two of them led their guests out of the burning house and into the garden, some distance away from the danger of flying sparks.

31

The servants lifted the massive table and carried it down the steps and out onto the terrace, and some guests reported later that not even a drop of water was spilled on the damask cloth.

"Shall I bring candles or lamps?" a servant asked.

"No," replied Tattnall. "Firelight from Bonaventure will illumine our table."

So while the great house burned, the dinner party continued beneath the oak trees in the garden.

Before the guests departed, they drank toasts to Bonaventure, to its rich memories. There was a toast, too, to the final dinner party there.

"May the joy of this occasion never end," the gentleman proposed. It seemed a strange toast on such a night.

The guests drank the toast, and then, following the lead of their host, they shattered their glasses against the trunks of the Bonaventure oaks.

It has been a long time, perhaps a hundred and seventy-five years, since Bonaventure burned.

The oak trees are still there, their gnarled limbs softened by streamers of moss, but now they shade not a grand manor house and its formal gardens but the graves of Savannah's dead. The site is still called Bonaventure, but another word has been added—cemetery. Bonaventure Cemetery.

Here buried in their family plot are Mr. and Mrs. Josiah Tattnall, Jr., ("An honest man rich in the estimation of all who knew him," his marker says) and their children: Josiah, a year and a half old; Mary M., eight, named for her great-grandmother; John M., his great-grandfather's namesake, who was almost four, and Baby Sally, six months old.

Here in the family plot are the Tattnall graves.

And here at Bonaventure people passing late at night still hear distinctly the sounds of a dinner party in progress: the clatter of dishes, the tinkle of silverware, the voices and laughter of guests, and then the shattering of crystal glasses.

Hearing these festive sounds, the passers-by nod and say, "It's still going on, the eternal dinner party at Bonaventure."

33

A Ghost For The Springer

The Springer Opera House in Columbus should, by rights, have its choice of ghosts. On no stage in the South has a more varied or more illustrious cast of characters appeared, and no theatre has been more closely bound to the entertainment and cultural life of Georgia than has the century-old Springer.

In the archives of the opera house are newspaper clippings, photographs, playbills, and programs chronicling the history of the Springer, but, unfortunately, in this accumulation of memorabilia there are no accounts of visitations by ghosts. Ghost lore at the Springer appears to be a neglected field. Or it was. Now, after decades of having shunned the Springer, there are definite indications that ghosts have arrived to haunt the building.

The theatre has long had the usual scary but logical-to-explain noises (vibrations from traffic, rats scurrying across the roof, pigeons trapped in upstairs rooms, and such), but people working in the empty Springer now tell of hearing mysterious music, snatches of melodies played by an unseen orchestra. There are recent accounts, too, of stage props being moved by ghostly intruders and of strange tampering with the third floor costume closets.

It does appear that, at last, the Springer has a ghost.

In the past, members of the Springer's governing body and persons closely connected with its productions have been slightly embarrassed and somewhat apologetic about their theatre's lack of a resident spirit. It is unthinkable, they agree, that a theatre as prideful of its past as is the Springer should be so completely neglected by representatives of the spirit world.

It has not made them happy to be reminded that almost all theatres of note have ghosts, not just plain ghosts but splendid spirits whose dramatic exploits provide exciting material worthy of presentation by a live theatrical troupe. There is, for example, the ghost in the theatre in nearby Auburn, Alabama, a ghost named Sydney who had become such an accepted and widely-known member of the Auburn Players that the theatre department awards are named for him, the Sydney Awards. Columbus theatre lovers have wearied of hearing about Sydney.

But if the sponsors and the patrons of the Springer envy the ghostly traditions of other theatres, they find solace in the knowledge that no other theatre in the South surpasses theirs in Victorian elegance or in the roster of illustrious personages who have appeared on their stage. From the time it opened in 1871 until it suffered the degradation of being converted into a movie house seventy years later, the Springer attracted the foremost theatrical, musical, oratorical, and ballet talent in the country.

Joseph Jefferson, Franklin Delano Roosevelt, Tom Thumb, Maude Adams, John L. Sullivan, Ethel Barrymore, Irving Berlin, Buffalo Bill Cody, William S. Hart, Victor Herbert, William Jennings Bryan, Will Rogers, Booker T. Washington, Oscar Wilde, Edwin Booth, Fritz Kreisler, Ted

Shawn, Ruth St. Dennis—the list goes on and on. They all appeared at the Springer, and the spirit of any one of them would have been welcomed inside the old play house.

However, persons who have studied the recent manifestations believe that it is Edwin Booth who has returned, Booth the Shakespearean master protesting the theatre's failure to present the play which made him famous.

The Springer Opera House had been open for five years when Edwin Booth appeared there in the role of Hamlet. The date was February 15, 1876. Edwin Booth had played Shakespeare in Columbus earlier, appearing with his brother, John Wilkes Booth, during the late 1850s, before the Springer was built. He had found Columbus audiences unusually appreciative of his classical acting, and he had close friends in the city, but he was apprehensive about returning there.

"Will they accept me now?" he asked. "Will I be applauded for my portrayal of Hamlet or will I be scorned as the brother of John Wilkes Booth, the assassin?"

He wrote to John J. Burrus, Sr., manager of the Springer, asking his advice about scheduling Columbus on his southern tour.

"Come," Burrus advised him. "You will be accepted for your fine acting." Burrus was right.

His admirers were present at the station when the railway car which brought the theatrical group from New York was moved onto a siding. They saw a slight, rather aloof man come down the steps of the car and shake hands with the theatre manager and other officials waiting there to welcome him. His hair was black and quite long, so long that it billowed beneath the brim of his silk hat and rested on the fur collar of his coat.

With Booth was his second wife, Mary McVicker Booth, who even then was displaying symptoms of the madness that

37

was to wreck her life. She had insisted on accompanying her husband on this southern tour (the tour was arranged by John T. Ford who was to pay Booth $30,000 for fifty performances), but her presence created many problems. She found it impossible to sleep while the train was in motion, so, for her benefit, the car in which she and Booth traveled had to be placed on a siding each night. This nightly delay tended to make scheduling difficult for the tour manager.

The Springer was filled to capacity that February 15, the lower floor, the two balconies, and the eighteen boxes, as residents from throughout the Valley came to see Edwin Booth's portrayal of Hamlet. Booth, it is reported, was delighted with the reception accorded him in Columbus, and he was most complimentary of the Springer Opera House.

Theatre lovers in Columbus had long wanted such a place of entertainment as the Springer, for theatre in Columbus is nearly as old as the town itself. Almost before the first settlers had found shelter, back in 1828, a traveling theatrical company put on a show in Columbus, and it was only a few months later that an entrepreneur named Sol Smith erected a rough log building to house the presentation of a historical drama called *Pizarro*.

The audience on that opening night failed to learn much about the Spanish conqueror, however. The cast of extras, genuine Creek Indians imported from across the Chattahoochee to play the parts of Peruvian warriors, consumed their pay (a glass of whiskey) before instead of after the show, prompting them to put on a wild performance which terrified the other actors and delighted the audience.

Later plays were somewhat more orderly but decidedly less exciting. Minstrels, operas, circuses, melodramas, and performances of the classics were all a part of Columbus' entertainment and cultural legacy, but no theatre in the growing city was adequate for the presentations.

Preliminary plans for a new theatre had been made in the late 1850s, but with the outbreak of the War the South had to concentrate on armament and fighting forces rather than on culture and entertainment. There was no talk of a new theatre for several years.

The period of Reconstruction would seem an unlikely time for the leaders of a Georgia city to be planning the construction of an elegant theatre, but in June of 1869 backers of the project had begun to raise money for the building and had even selected the site. Their theatre, they decided, would be placed on one of Columbus' busiest corners, the intersection of First Avenue and Tenth Street where Francis J. Springer's grocery business stood.

Mr. Springer, who had come to Columbus from Alsace before the War, was quite willing to sacrifice his business location, and in May, 1870, the demolition of his store began. Mr. Springer, in fact, was one of the prime promoters of the theatre project. Although he could certainly have invested his money more profitably, he entered into an agreement to help finance the construction of the opera house with the understanding that when he had paid the obligation, the ownership of the structure would go to him and to his heirs.

And so construction of the three-story brick building began. The opera house itself measured one hundred feet long by eighty feet wide and sixty feet deep, quite the largest in that part of Georgia. On the parquet or lower floor were rows of cane-bottomed chairs, described as quite fine, while common pine benches with cast iron supports provided seating for spectators in the double galleries. The space above the stage was designed, as is customary, for the flies and backdrops used in creating illusions of reality, and the whole was illumined by gas lamps.

The opera house had the center location, and extending along Tenth Street and along First Avenue were shops and stores (Mr. Springer moved his retail and wholesale grocery business back into the building). On the upper floors were hotel rooms.

No theatre has been more closely bound to the entertainment and cultural life of Georgia than has the century-old Springer.

The brass sign out front was emblazoned "Springer Hotel and Opera House."

On February 21, 1871, the Springer Opera House was officially opened with a concert presented by members of the Trinity Episcopal Church—still a neighbor of the Springer—to help raise money for a new building. The painters had provided a palace scene as background for the concert, and the newspaper reviewer described it as "so artistically gotten up as to make the illusion almost perfect."

The six hundred or so patrons who attended the opening concert only half filled the opera house. Attendance would have been greater, it was explained, had not four other churches in the city been engaged in protracted meetings at the time, meetings which claimed the loyal presence of church members who otherwise would have gone to the Episcopal concert.

Either the protracted meetings had ended or the loyalty had dwindled by the following week when Katie Putnam brought her theatrical troupe to the Springer. For a solid week Katie and her performers played before packed houses as they acted out *The Little Detective, Lady of Lyons, Household Treasure, The Old Curiosity Shop*, and *Pocahontas.*

Thus the Springer Opera House was well launched by the time Edwin Booth arrived in mid-February, 1876, to play Hamlet. There was not a seat to be had when Booth, clad in his inky cloak, appeared on stage, and by the time the curtain rose on Act III, the poignant quality of Booth's Hamlet had so touched and enraptured the audience that spectators waited in almost eerie silence for him to speak, "To be, or not to be—"

Years later, members of that audience still treasured the memory of that night, and their voices were touched with reverence as they told their children and their grandchildren,

"I saw Edwin Booth play Hamlet."

Perhaps it is significant that the play which brought Edwin Booth his greatest fame dealt with ghosts, and certainly it is appropriate that this play, *Hamlet*, is the one he chose to present at the Springer.

For surely it is the ghost of Edwin Booth who unlocks the costume closet at the Springer and rummages through the racks of garments seeking the proper attire for the players in *Hamlet*. Edwin Booth, though he sometimes protested that he was weary of it, revered the role of Hamlet, and it must distress him that the players in the reclaimed and restored Springer have not included *Hamlet* in their repertoire.

Since the Springer was literally snatched from the grasp of demolition crews in 1963 (it had been dark and boarded up for six years), the theatre has been restored to its red plush and gilt splendor. Chandeliers light the eighteen private boxes, and garlands of tulip lights, salvaged from rubble found in the basement, outline the graceful curves of the balconies. But these refinements mean little to a spirit clamoring for a performance of *Hamlet*.

While work on the theatre itself has been virtually completed, other parts of the building await renovation or possible conversion into office space and shops. Meantime, the long corridors of hotel rooms with their numbered doors serve as storage space for props and for costumes. It is in the costume area that the Springer's ghost is active.

A fire wall with a heavy metal door seals off the costume wing from the rest of the theatre building. This door is kept locked, and only authorized personnel are permitted to turn the key in the padlock and enter.

The key itself hangs in a sacrosanct spot in the business office. But it was not in its designated place when a theatre official, working alone in the building, needed it to check on some costumes. The key was gone. She searched the desk

The padlock was unlocked—and the hasp was gently swaying back and forth.

thoroughly, and then she walked up the stairs to see if perhaps someone had left the key in the lock. No one had. The door was securely locked.

So back down the stairs she went. When she reached the office, there in the middle of the bare desk lay the key. Nobody had entered the building, and nobody had left.

She took the key, though she admitted being hesitant about touching it, and trudged upstairs again. This time she found the padlock unlocked—and the hasp was gently swaying back and forth.

Somebody, some unseen hands, had opened the lock only seconds earlier, the same somebody who had conducted a neat but futile search through the rooms with their racks of costumes. It must have been Edwin Booth, persons who know of the incident say, hoping to find costumes for *Hamlet.* The key, first missing and then later placed in plain view, the swinging hasp, the disarranged costumes were all part of Booth's plan to make theatre personnel aware of his presence, to focus their attention on reviving his play, his *Hamlet,* they speculate.

Is Edwin Booth also responsible for the strange, ethereal music that sometimes fills the theatre? People who have heard the music say it is tender, soothing, lacking a definite melody yet melodic.

"There's nothing frightening about it," they say. "Sometimes when you're working in the Springer you're aware of being surrounded by music—coming from the empty orchestra pit maybe, maybe coming from nowhere. Later, though you listen closely, you can't quite recall the tune or even the rhythm. The lovely, peaceful sounds—the mood—are all you remember."

Edwin Booth loved such music. As a boy, Edwin played soft music to soothe his father, Junius Brutus Booth, during those times when the elder Booth was possessed by madness.

Edwin Booth knew, too, the hypnotic effect music could produce in setting the mood for a play.

The music heard in the Springer Opera House would provide a perfect background for the soliloquies of Hamlet.

The Ghost Of
Andersonville

The three friends had attended a civic club meeting in Americus and were returning home, driving along Georgia Highway 49, a road quite familiar to each of them. It was late December, 1971.

They had stayed after the meeting to chat with friends, and the time had slipped by faster than they had realized. Now it was nearly midnight, and Mrs. Louise Campbell, who was driving, was intent on reaching home as quickly as was safely possible. Her companions, Mr. and Mrs. Norman Gerritsen, lived in Oglethorpe, so after she had taken them home, Mrs. Campbell would be driving alone to Perry. Although she was not afraid, Mrs. Campbell did not particularly like to be alone on the road so late at night.

She was concentrating on her driving, watching the road closely, as the car moved north through Sumter County. She drove this route often, and, as she usually did, she mentally crossed off the landmarks as she passed, the churches, homes, stores, and communities that marked her homeward progress.

She had just crossed off Andersonville National Cemetery with its historic markers and its tall fences (the identical rows

47

The identical rows of identical gravestones at Andersonville.

of identical gravestones were not visible from the highway) when she saw something she had never seen before. Standing beside the road was a man in military uniform. He had on an overcoat, long and full, and his cap touched the coat's turned-up collar. Even her quick look at the man gave Mrs. Campbell an uneasy feeling, a sense of strangeness as though she had been snatched from the present and catapulted back in time.

She braked the car, though she was not sure why, as she asked, "Did you see—"'

"Yes," Gerritsen interrupted. "I saw that man in the strange uniform. I saw him." Gerritsen was sitting on the right side of the car and thus had had a close view of the soldier. He had turned his head and was looking backward to verify what he had seen when Mrs. Campbell asked her question.

"Go back," he urged.

Mrs. Campbell was already turning the car around, and moments later they were back at the spot where they had seen the figure.

Nobody was there.

Mrs. Campbell drove down the road a short distance, thinking perhaps the man might have walked in that direction, but there was no sign of anyone.

Now the puzzle of the soldier's disappearance became as mystifying as did his original appearance.

"Where could he have gone?" Mrs. Gerritsen asked. She had not seen the figure (she was sitting in the middle on the front seat), but she had been hurriedly told about the sighting and had scanned the roadside hoping for a glimpse of the man as the trio returned to the scene.

"He couldn't possibly have got out of sight so quickly," Gerritsen said. "It was only two or three minutes at most from the time we saw him and the time we got back. He didn't walk along the highway, or we would have seen him. He didn't cross the road—I was looking back. He couldn't have got into the cemetery, not over that tall fence. His long coat would have snagged on the barbed wire around the top if he had tried to climb over."

"You noticed the coat, too?" Mrs. Campbell asked.

"Yes," Gerritsen replied, trying hard to recall exactly what he had seen. "Yes, he had on an overcoat, a military coat of some kind, and a cap. I couldn't see the color, but the uniform looked odd and old, like it might have come out of the Civil War period." He paused. "You don't suppose—surely not!"

"If you're thinking that we saw a ghost, I agree with you," Mrs. Campbell said. "We both saw it—or him—standing right there, and now the figure has gone. Vanished. Isn't that how ghosts do? This whole thing has made me feel eerie and uncomfortable. I'll be glad to get home."

"Do you really suppose you saw a ghost?" Mrs. Gerritsen asked. "Whose ghost was it?" She was disappointed that she had not seen even a glimpse of the elusive military man, and she kept wishing she had been looking out the car window at the right moment. She felt sure that if she had seen the solitary soldier she would have noticed details about his appearance that her husband and Mrs. Campbell failed to observe.

"Whose ghost was it?" she asked again.

"I don't know," her husband answered. "It could have been the ghost of so many people here at Andersonville. So many."

During the next few days theories as to the identity of the ghost grew in number and variety as the trio shared accounts of their strange experience with friends. Most of their listeners believed that they had seen the ghost of a Yankee soldier, one of the thousands of prisoners who died inside the

Providence Spring is still there.

Andersonville stockade, victims of malnutrition, measles, typhoid, dysentery, and despair during the final miserable months of the war.

"But why," someone asked, "out of all the men who died there—were there really 13,000 deaths—out of all those men, why would the ghost of only one return?"

Again there were theories, speculation.

"Perhaps," suggested a history student, "it was the ghost of the thirsty prisoner whose prayers for water were answered by the spring of pure, cold water that burst forth at

51

his feet. Perhaps he came back to see if his spring—Providence Spring as the prisoners called it—is still there."

"The spring's still there all right," someone else spoke up, "but I doubt that he'd recognize it. It has a permanent shelter over it, and the water is piped outside to a drinking fountain. I believe though," he added, "there's a sign at the fountain warning that the water isn't safe to drink!"

His listeners laughed, grateful for a touch of humor to shake from their thoughts the images of suffering that talk of Andersonville conjured up.

Then someone suggested, mainly in jest, that the ghost could be the spirit of the freedom-minded prisoner whose escape tunnel surfaced right in the middle of a Confederate campfire.

"When the soldier pushed up through the ground that night, fire and hot coals and Confederates scattered every which way. The Confederate guards, most of them just young boys, thought sure the Devil was coming up after them!"

Again they laughed.

There were other suggestions, including the proposal that the ghost was one of the ringleaders of the "Andersonville Raiders," a gang of Yankee thugs whose reign of terror inside the prison was broken only after six of them were hanged.

It was a serious student of ghost lore who suggested that the trio had seen the tormented spirit of Captain Henry Wirz, commander of the inner prison from April 12, 1864, to May 7, 1865. Many spirits, the student pointed out, return after death to try to clear their reputations. Captain Wirz would have reason to return on such a mission.

Somehow Wirz, the Swiss immigrant who was given a wretched and intolerable assignment during the final months of the war, became for Northerners the very embodiment of evil. On him they heaped their hatred, and at him they hurled charges of being responsible for the deplorable conditions not only at Andersonville but also wherever their men had suffered and died in prison.

There were other prisons, other officers who failed to provide humane treatment for prisoners in their care, but it was the name Wirz that Northerners knew. Wirz. Wirz. Wirz.

They said he was ignorant and uneducated, though he held degrees from medical colleges in Paris and Berlin and spoke three languages (French, German, and English) fluently.

They said he was indifferent to the plight of the prisoners though he arranged for a delegation from Andersonville to go to Washington to plead with federal officials to reinstate the prisoner exchange program.

They said he had no comprehension of physical discomfort though he lived with the constant pain of a useless right arm, shattered in the Battle of Seven Pines.

They said he was a wholesale murderer though he was never officially linked with the death of a single prisoner.

They said he was a lying coward though he faced death bravely rather than swear to a falsehood that would have saved his life.

In his defense Wirz could point out that Andersonville was already a miserable, stinking hellhole when he arrived there in the spring of 1864. More than 30,000 men were penned in an enclosure designed to accommodate 8,000 to 10,000. The stream with a deceptively lovely name, Sweetwater Creek, that was to furnish drinking water for the prisoners had become a foul sewer. The planned barracks had never been built, and flimsy tents plus a few adobe and log shebangs provided the prisoners' only protection from the searing summer sun, the penetrating winter chill, and the drenching rains that mired the site in all seasons.

The rations may have been ample to prevent or to postpone starvation, but the food was vermin-filled, moldy and unvaried. Certainly it did nothing to relieve the twin curses of the camp: scurvy and dysentery.

That was the way things were when Captain Wirz arrived at Andersonville. He did not create the situation; it was foisted off on him, and, later, he could never understand why he should have been blamed and hated for conditions he was powerless to correct. But he was.

Almost a month after General Robert E. Lee's surrender to General U. S. Grant in Virginia, federal officers came to Captain Wirz' home at Andersonville (he and his family lived in the village, some distance from the prison) to escort him to General J. H. Wilson's headquarters in Macon.

The captain was not alarmed at this procedure, but his wife was apprehensive, fearful of what the officers might do to her husband. Wirz tried to reassure her that he was in no real danger and that he would soon be home again.

"These officers are gentlemen, courteous and refined," he told his wife. "You know how graciously they accepted your invitation to join us at dinner, and, though we had precious little to share with them, they thanked you for your hospitality. Men such as that will do me no harm.

"Naturally General Wilson wants an official report on the conduct of the prison here. I will take my records with me and go over them with him. Don't worry. I'll be back soon."

At first it seemed that Captain Wirz' assessment of the situation was correct. He presented the prison records to General Wilson, and for about two hours the general questioned him about conditions at Andersonville. Then, apparently satisfied that the Confederate commander was not guilty of criminal behavior, General Wilson dismissed him.

"You may go home to your family," General Wilson told the captain.

The two men shook hands, and Captain Wirz went to the station to await the arrival of a train to Andersonville.

Train schedules had not returned to normal—nothing

had—and Captain Wirz learned that his train would be several hours late. It was a most unfortunate delay for Captain Wirz.

He waited impatiently as the hours passed, wanting to get home to relieve his wife's anxiety. He was about to doze, being weary from the mental ordeal of his interview with General Wilson and from the long delay in the station, when a federal officer walked up to him, took him into custody, and put him under guard.

Although General Wilson had apparently accepted Captain Wirz' version of his role in the administration of Andersonville, public indignation in the North seems to have pressured General Wilson's superiors to order him to produce a man who could be charged with the alleged crimes at the Confederate prison. It was easy for him to produce Captain Wirz.

The captain was sent to Washington where he was placed in the Old Capitol Prison on May 10, 1865. For three months he was held prisoner while the government prepared its case against him, and for three months the Northern press pictured him as the "greatest criminal of all time."

He was charged with conspiring with Jefferson Davis and other Confederate officers to "impair and injure the health and to destroy the lives by subjecting to great torture and suffering" a large number of federal prisoners and with the deliberate murder of eleven unnamed Union soldiers.

The trial began on August 25, 1865. Accounts of that trial say that the star witness against Captain Wirz was a young man named Felix de la Baume who added credence to his testimony by claiming to be a nephew of General LaFayette.

Baume, the reports say, held the crowd at the trial spellbound for hours as he described conditions at Andersonville and told of Wirz' "inhuman cruelty" to prisoners there.

After he had given his damaging testimony against the

defendant and after he had also been given a position in the Interior Department, it was learned that this supposedly expert witness was not a kinsman of LaFayette but was, in fact, a deserter from the Union Army.

Nevertheless, Wirz was found guilty and was sentenced to be hanged. Offers were made of clemency or possibly even of pardon if he would sign statements implicating Jefferson Davis in the conspiracy, but he would not.

Captain Henry Wirz was hanged in Washington on November 10, 1865. He was the only Confederate officer ever convicted and executed for war crimes.

A few hours before his death the condemned man wrote a letter to a friend in which he said,

"Please help my poor family, my dear wife and children. War, cruelest war, has swept everything from me, and today my wife and children are beggars. My life is demanded as an atonement. I am willing to give it, and after a while I will be judged differently from what I am now."

Was it the ghost of Captain Henry Wirz that Mrs. Campbell and Mr. Gerritsen saw? Is his spirit wandering restlessly around Andersonville hoping to clear his name, hoping to "be judged differently?"

"My life is demanded as an atonement," Captain Wirz wrote.

CAPTAIN HENRY WIRZ
1823 - 1865

Captain Henry Wirz, under the immediate command of Brigadier-General John H. Winder, C.S.A., absent on sick leave, August 1864, commanded the inner prison at Camp Sumter, April 12, 1864 to May 7, 1865. To the best of his ability he tried to obtain food and medicine for Federal prisoners and permitted some to go to Washington in a futile attempt to get prisoners exchanged. He was tried for failure to provide food and medicines for Federals imprisoned here - though his guards ate the same food - and mortality was as high among Confederate guards as among prisoners. Of him, Eliza Frances Andrews, Georgia writer, said, "Had he been an angel from heaven, he could not have changed the pitiful tale of privation and hunger unless he had possessed the power to repeat the miracle of the loaves and fishes." Refusing to implicate others, he gave his life for the South, November 10, 1865.

129-2   GEORGIA HISTORICAL COMMISSION   1956

The Wickedest Man In Georgia

They say Sherman did not burn Milledgeville because so many Masons lived there, and they say he did not take S. Walker's cotton because Walker told him where other planters in the county had hidden their bales of fiber.

Nobody ever actually proved that Walker was in cahoots with the Yankees and nobody ever openly accused him of it, but folks in Milledgeville whispered about it and cogitated about it and added it to the list of Walker's evil deeds.

It was a long list.

They used to say that even the Devil was scared of S. Walker. There was a joke they used to tell in Milledgeville, behind his back of course, about Walker and the Devil. They said one of the imps down in hell saw the Devil sitting on a big black washpot, a pot that had been turned over. A good bit later when the imp passed by that way again, the Devil was still sitting there on the washpot.

"What you doing just sitting there, Devil? Why ain't you busy rounding up folks for hell?" the imp asked.

"Well," the Devil replied, "I've got S. Walker under this washpot, and I'm scared if I get up he'll get loose and tear up hell."

They said S. Walker was the wickedest man in Georgia, and they said he was not scared of anything or anybody except the ghost of his son. Some folks said Walker killed his son. Other folks, maybe a little more charitable, said Walker did not actually kill his son with his own two hands but that you might say he was responsible for the boy's death.

S. Walker moved to Milledgeville about the time the War ended. He had been living on a plantation up near Eatonton, right close by, so everybody in Milledgeville pretty well knew what his reputation was even before he moved there. He had not been in Milledgeville long, either, before they agreed he was just as bad as they had heard he was.

He brought his third wife and son, Josiah, with him to Milledgeville. That wife was not Josiah's mother. His mother had died after childbirth. There were some ugly rumors after Mrs. Walker (his first wife) died, especially after Walker took over her big plantation. It was worth a lot of money.

His second wife died under peculiar and right suspicious circumstances, too, folks said, but nobody knew the details. The third Mrs. Walker was considered to be a mighty brave or a mighty foolish woman to marry a man so careless with his wives.

Mrs. Walker, the third, did not have any children, but she and Walker were raising a niece, a little girl named Alice. Walker loved Alice, really loved her, in a sweet, gentle way.

That was a peculiar thing about Walker. Mixed in with all his meanness, he had little patches of goodness.

Take his flowers, for instance.

When he bought that big house at the corner of Jefferson and McIntosh Streets, right away he added a conservatory. It seemed all out of character for S. Walker to build a room just to raise flowers in, but he did.

And everybody agreed that he grew the prettiest roses in

60

town. In the spring when Walker's roses were blooming, it looked like a parade going past his garden some afternoons with so many folks walking by to admire the blossoms. He prettied up his sidewalk, too, with big red paving blocks and with ornamental posts and urns set in the high cement coping around his garden.

The house where Walker lived had been built by his grandmother. She favored the Greek Revival style, mighty popular in Milledgeville then, with tall white columns and a balcony on the front. Walker was not much on Greek Revival. When he got the house, he took down the columns and the balcony, and he built a narrow porch across the front and down one side of the house. He had bannisters put on his porch, and he added some other fancy touches, sort of early Victorian.

In his journeying around, Walker had seen a few houses with mansard roofs, and they stuck in his mind, so he went back to Milledgeville and put one on his house. He did not bother to take the old roof off: he just nailed the mansard roof on top of it.

Somewhere else he saw a house with an eight-sided room in it. Pretty soon Walker had one in his house, too. His room was twenty feet across from wall to wall and sixteen feet high, and it had four doors, two French windows, a curved fireplace, and a pointed copper roof.

While he was building the house, Walker added some secret closets close to his bedroom. There were a heap of rumors about what was in those closets—turned out the closets themselves were not secret, just what was in them was. It was pretty well accepted as fact that costumes or uniforms, some of them all white, were stored in the closets. They were handy in case he happened to need them during the night, folks said.

For maybe ten years after he moved in the house Walker

S. Walker added to and changed and remodeled this old house in Milledgeville.

was busy doing things to it, adding to and tearing out and rearranging. Walker had time for his building and his gardening and such because he did not work. At least he did not have to go to a store or an office every day like most men did. He had some plantations, but he was only interested in the money they made, so he hired overseers to run them. The overseers stayed only as long as they showed a profit.

Mostly Walker's wealth came from lending money and foreclosing mortgages. He did a lot of both. That is how he got the old Whittaker plantation over across the river. At least folks say Captain Whittaker lost his land because he thought Walker was a gentleman. He should have known better.

Anyhow, folks said Captain Whittaker borrowed $2,000 from Walker one spring to buy fertilizer for his cotton. He promised to pay back the loan, plus a sizable interest, when he sold his cotton. The date he was supposed to pay was set down in the paper he signed when he got the fertilizer money.

Well, it seems Captain Whittaker made a good crop of cotton (he owned some fine land), and he had it ginned and baled and loaded on wagons ready to bring to Milledgeville to sell. It was close to time for him to pay off his loan from Walker. Captain Whittaker was not sure exactly what day the note was due (he had misplaced his papers), but he knew it was soon.

Before he got his wagons started toward town, a bad storm came up. He did not want to get his cotton wet, so Captain Whittaker kept his loaded cotton wagons under sheds.

It rained and it rained and it rained. Did not even slack up for three or four days. All that hard rain made the Oconee rise fast. It rose right on up over the bridge between the plantation and Milledgeville, so that Captain Whittaker could not take his cotton to town until the river went down.

Soon as it was safe to cross the bridge, Captain Whittaker took his cotton to Milledgeville and sold it and carried the money right straight to Walker.

"Good morning," he said, smiling, "I've come to pay my note." He reached for his wallet.

"Sorry, Captain," Walker said. He was not smiling. "Your note was due yesterday. I've already foreclosed the mortgage. One of my overseers is on his way over there to take charge now."

That is the sort of man S. Walker was.

Not long after Walker took the Whittaker plantation, his son, Josiah, came home from Mercer College. Some kind of fever had broken out among the students—a few of the young men had died—and the officials had closed the school. Temporarily, of course.

Walker was not pleased at all to have his boy come home. The two of them never had gotten along, not even when Josiah was little. After the boy got old enough and big enough to stand up to his father, they used to have some bad arguments. Walker, folks who heard their fusses reported, told the boy more than once, "You should have died with your mother!"

That is how it was between Walker and his son. Even when Walker said those things to him, though, Josiah tried to be respectful and be a good son and please his father, but he never could.

So when Josiah came home from Mercer, Walker was upset. He did not like having the boy around the house: he saw too much and asked too many questions.

"Long as you're home, you might as well be useful, not spend all your time reading," Walker greeted his son. "There's work needs doing over at the Whittaker place. Ride on over there and tell the overseer I sent you."

Josiah took some old clothes and some books (Walker

never could understand why Josiah liked books) and rode across the river to the plantation.

By early afternoon Josiah was back home in Milledgeville. His stepmother heard him stumble up the stairs to his room, and she went to see about him.

"I'm sick, real sick," Josiah mumbled. He fell onto the bed.

His stepmother pulled off his boots for him and put a pillow under his head. She sent Alice to get a pan of cold water and a washrag so she could bathe his face. His skin felt hot and dry, and there was a breaking out on his arms.

Walker saw Josiah's horse in the barn, and he came blustering into the house to find out why his son had come back home.

"The boy's sick," Mrs. Walker said. "He's real sick."

"He's not sick—he's lazy," Walker answered. All the way up the stairs to Josiah's room he kept shouting about how Josiah was lazy and was playing like he was sick so he would not have to work on the plantation.

"Get up from there!" Walker ordered Josiah. He sounded real mad. And mean, too.

Josiah tried to raise up, but he fell right back on the pillow.

"I'm sick, Papa. And I'm scared. Please get a doctor. Please," the boy begged. He was too weak to talk loud or to say much.

"That I will not!" Walker told him. "I'll not waste money on a doctor when you're not even sick."

He slammed the door.

"Stay out of the boy's room," he told Mrs. Walker and Alice. "When he gets hungry enough and thirsty enough, he'll get up and come downstairs. He's just putting on. Don't you go traipsing up there waiting on him."

Mrs. Walker generally did what her husband told her to do,

65

but she could not stand to hear Josiah cry out for water, and she took it to him when her husband was away from the house. Josiah did not beg for water except when he was delirious. Other times he just lay there and stared.

Two or three times when Mrs. Walker was in his room he asked her to tell his father he needed a doctor, but the messages did not do any good. They just made Walker madder and more stubborn.

On the third day that Josiah was sick Mrs. Walker got bold, and she told her husband, "You must get a doctor. Josiah is dying."

That sort of scared Walker. He was already feeling a little uncomfortable—not guilty, just uncomfortable—about maybe neglecting his boy, so he started upstairs to see about him.

Walker had just stepped on the landing of the stair when the door to Josiah's room opened. Josiah steadied himself by holding on to the door facing. Then he reached out for the post at the head of the stairs.

He looked straight at his father, his eyes all glassy and sunken, and he said,

"Papa, you see—"

Before he could finish whatever it was he wanted to say, Josiah collapsed and tumbled down the steps to the landing where Walker stood.

"My God!" Walker screamed. "Get a doctor quick!"

It was too late then.

Josiah was dead.

A few days later Mrs. Walker and Alice got sick. Walker sent for the doctor right away, and Walker himself waited on them the best he knew how, bathing their foreheads and bringing them water and such, but they both died.

Walker was left alone in the big house with the mansard roof and the eight-sided room and the secret closets.

He was not altogether alone though because the ghost of

his boy, Josiah, kept coming back to haunt him.

They say sometimes Walker would start up the stairs, and he would look and there would be Josiah standing in the doorway of his bedroom staring at him. It finally got so bad, Walker seeing Josiah so plain and so often, that Walker closed off the upstairs and would not go up there for the longest kind of time.

At night lots of times Walker would wake up hearing Josiah calling for water and begging for a doctor.

It got to where Walker did not like to go home at all. He took to playing cards at night, and he would stay out as late as anybody would stay to play with him.

One night Walker was playing setback with some friends in the lobby of the old Baldwin Hotel. Actually they were not exactly friends Walker was playing with, but they were the closest thing he had to friends. They were all relaxed and were having a good time when all of a sudden Walker threw down his cards and yelled,

"My God! Look behind you—my boy is standing there!"

Nobody else saw whatever it was that upset Walker, but the other card players knew in all reason that something had been there in that lobby. They said they never saw a grown man as pale and as trembly and all to pieces as Walker was.

But Walker's worst torment came those long days and nights just before he died. It was a stroke that killed him. They said Josiah's ghost came and stood at the foot of Walker's death bed. He, the ghost, just stood there and looked at Walker. Never said a word, just stared.

Walker screamed and cried and begged for forgiveness. He would plead, "Don't look at me! Josiah, please don't look at me!" And he would add, "I didn't know you were sick, Josiah. I would have sent for the doctor if I'd known. Please forgive me." And then he would start again begging Josiah not to look at him.

He was still begging for forgiveness when he died.

The big house on the corner of Jefferson and McIntosh streets looks much the same as it did when the Walkers lived there. It still has the mansard roof and the eight-sided room and the Victorian porch.

It still has ghosts, too.

People living there still hear footsteps on the stairs, and they know that, too late, S. Walker is going up to see about his son. And then they hear other steps, lighter steps, in the hall, and a thud on the landing.

It is a pitiful sound.

People still hear footsteps on the stairs and a thud on the landing.

Footsteps At Orna Villa

Orna Villa is filled with noises, not just the usual creaking and settling of ancient timbers but sounds that echo like village gossip the old tales of family dissension and frustration.

Doors slam. Pictures fall from walls. Footsteps pace restlessly back and forth. And a squeaking chair rocks late into the night.

Even the heavy locks (they bear the imprint of English ironmongers of the 1790s) do not keep the doors from slamming, and the sturdiest nails fail to hold wall hangings in place. Providing a background for these sudden noises of slamming and crashing, the troubled pacing across the back porch and the steady rhythm of the rocker have continued at Orna Villa for nearly a century.

Orna Villa is the oldest house in Oxford, Georgia, a two-story frame structure with four plain square columns across the front. Dr. Alexander Means, Oxford's most distinguished citizen, did not build the house; he acquired the property in the mid-1830s and began a continuing series of improvements and enlargements to accommodate his growing

71

family.

He was well settled in the house by 1837 when Georgia Methodists bought 1,452 acres adjoining his home site for the purpose of building a college and a town. The founders called the college Emory in memory of Methodist Bishop John Emory, and they named the town Oxford in honor of the English university where John and Charles Wesley, founders of Methodism, were educated.

Dr. Means welcomed the expansion of church-sponsored education, and he was one of the select group of men who planned and promoted the project. He had already, at the age of 36, gained recognition as a pioneer educator in the field of natural science and as an educational administrator, so when the college opened, he was a member of the original faculty. Later he was to serve for one year as president of the institution.

It is doubtful that Dr. Means at this time, or at any other time, believed in ghosts. However, his neighbors and many of his learned colleagues would have considered a belief in spirits more normal than what he did believe in: Dr. Means actually believed and taught that electricity would some day be used to light cities and to propel cars!

He conducted experiments with electricity at Orna Villa and in his laboratory at Emory College. As a result of these experiments, he is credited with having demonstrated a workable incandescent bulb to a gathering of leading Atlanta citizens in June, 1858.

Thomas Edison, the genius who later perfected the light bulb, was only a boy of eleven when Dr. Means astounded his Atlanta audience with what was described as "an illumination of such brightness that it put to shame the new gaslights of which Atlanta was so proud."

Most of the residents of Oxford did not understand his experiment or his conception of the uses of electricity, but

72

they respected Dr. Means too much to scoff at him openly. Many of them did consider his theories—and he himself—a "bit queer."

"He's smart," they would say. "Too smart, maybe. Reads too much. Must get some mighty peculiar notions out of those books he reads."

For Dr. Means did read consistently and widely. He read books on biology, physics, and chemistry (he was a scientist), on religion and theology (he was a licensed Methodist minister), on medicine and pharmacy (he was a medical doctor with a degree from Transylvania, Kentucky, University's School of Medicine), on literature (he wrote poetry), and on history and philosophy (he tried to understand the present by measuring it against the past).

There was never enough time in the day for all the reading he wanted to do, so Dr. Means used to stay up with his books very late at night. He sat in a rocking chair in his upstairs bedroom and read, read, read long after other members of the household were asleep. When, after several hours of reading, he felt himself getting drowsy, he rocked vigorously to keep from falling asleep.

So, some people believe, the sound of a rocking chair squeaking in a long vacant room at Orna Villa is the ghost of Dr. Means trying to catch up on his reading.

There is disagreement about the footsteps, definitely those of a man, which for years pounded up and down the long back porch at Orna Villa. Many occupants of the house have heard the footsteps (some of them have even been awakened by the noise), but they are not sure whether the phantom pacer is Tobe Means or his brother, Olin.

Tobe was the rebel, the non-conformist, the Bohemian in the family. Of all the nine children, Tobe was the least like his scholarly father. He shared none of his father's interests, and it seemed that their every conversation ended in a

73

quarrel.

Their bitterest disagreements were about Tobe's education.

Tobe had no desire to become a preacher or a lawyer or a doctor, so he saw no need to attend college. He wanted to travel and see the world.

"I don't want to read about things in books. I want to go see them for myself," Tobe would say.

His father in speaking of Tobe would sometimes say sadly, "Tobe is my son who knows how to read—but doesn't."

Tobe's initial announcement that he was not going to college brought a reaction of shocked disbelief from his father.

"Not go to college? Of course you'll go! To decline the privilege of a good education is unthinkable, almost sinful," Dr. Means told Tobe. He respected and valued education so highly and he had encountered such difficulties in getting his own schooling that the idea of a young man actually refusing to attend college confounded and angered him.

Tobe not only rebelled at attending college but went further and proposed that Dr. Means give him the money set aside for his education so that he could use it for traveling expenses on a proposed vagabond journey around the world.

"That money is for your education," Dr. Means would say each time Tobe brought up the subject.

"I will get my education by seeing the world," Tobe would reply.

These discussions always developed into bitter arguments. Tobe would storm from the room, slam the door and stamp up and down the back porch while he decried his father's lack of understanding.

It was after a particularly emotional and upsetting quarrel with his father that Tobe, angrier than he had ever been before, raged from the room, slamming the door behind him. On this occasion, the story goes, he did not give vent to his

74

angry frustration by walking back and forth on the porch. This night he saddled his horse and rode away, never to return.

After Tobe left, members of the family used to think every now and then that they heard him walking on the porch the way he used to do, and they would hurry to open the door and welcome him home. But there was never anybody on the porch.

So, with such a background, it is natural that some occupants of Orna Villa have credited—or blamed—Tobe with the ghostly nocturnal pacings.

Other people who have lived in the house say the footsteps herald the ghostly return of Dr. Olin Means, Tobe's brother.

Olin was very much like his father. He even had his father's small stature, his military bearing, his sharp blue eyes, and his courtly manner.

Just as his father had done, Olin studied medicine and received his degree from medical school. The two men differed though in that his father's interests and activities encompassed several fields while Olin was totally dedicated to the practice of medicine. He was an excellent doctor, and he was completely happy in the choice of his profession.

It came as a disturbing shock to Olin when he felt a call to preach.

It was a definite and persistent call, a call that nagged at his conscience and penetrated his thoughts and wrapped itself around his heart.

At first Olin hoped that he might be mistaken about what appeared to be a Divine interference in his life, and he tried to ignore it. But the feeling—or rather the definite knowledge—that he had been called to the ministry increased in intensity.

In his prayers he reminded God of the good he was accomplishing through his medical work, and he promised to increase his lay witnessing, but even this approach did not ease his conscience.

Olin had long conversations with his father about his problem, and the two men became closer than they had ever been before. They read Scripture and prayed together and discussed fully all choices of action open to Olin, but Dr. Means made no attempt to dictate what his son should do.

"Only you can decide what you believe God's will for your life is," Dr. Means would remind Olin, "The decision is yours."

Tormented by indecision, by his reluctance to give up the practice of medicine, Olin walked back and forth on the porch night after night wrestling with his conscience.

"I must have trod ten thousand miles and prayed ten thousand prayers, but I still cannot decide what to do," Olin confided to a friend. "I must make a decision soon!"

Dr. Olin Means suffered a sudden illness and died before that decision was ever made.

Thus it was that later occupants of Orna Villa, hearing footsteps on the back porch, would comment, "Olin's ghost is back tonight, still trying to decide if he will give up his practice of medicine to become a preacher. Listen to those troubled steps!"

The ghostly footsteps continued through the years and, though there was disagreement as to their source, became a treasured part of the Means' family tradition.

One of Dr. Means' granddaughters who was born at Orna Villa and who heard the footsteps of the invisible walker in her childhood wrote a poem about the experiences. Her poem, hardly up the the standard of the verse composed by her grandfather, contained these lines,

"He walks with assurance, his tread is not light;
This man from the dead seems to think he has right."

Even she did not identify the "man from the dead" as

76

The troubled pacings at Orna Villa have continued for nearly a century.

77

Tobe or Olin.

Recent residents of Orna Villa are not certain either whom they hear in the house—but they know that something or someone strange is there.

Back in the early 1940s when Mr. and Mrs. E. H. Rheberg bought the house, they employed local workmen to make certain renovations.

One cold morning Rheberg got up about dawn to go over plans for the day. He heard heavy steps on the back porch. A glance at the clock showed him it was entirely too early for the workmen to have arrived, but he reasoned that perhaps one of the men had come to deliver a message and, finding nobody awake, was walking briskly up and down the porch to keep warm.

"I'll let the fellow in before he freezes," Rheberg thought as he hurried to the back door.

The sound of the steps continued as Rheberg turned the key in the latch, but when he swung the door open, nobody was there.

Was it Tobe or was it Olin he heard? He never decided.

The back porch at Orna Villa has now been enclosed to make a family room, and this change may have discouraged or even thwarted the unseen walker.

However, the present owners, Mr. and Mrs. John Watterson, say that peculiar things, things for which there is no logical explanation, still happen there.

Doors open and close of their own accord, and occasionally a door will bang shut as though some unseen hand slammed it in anger.

A collection of guns, each gun mounted firmly in a bracket on the wall, all clattered to the floor on one occasion, landing in a heap around a glass-front bookcase without breaking the bookcase or damaging the guns.

Even the family canary appears to have been a victim of

ghostly activity. The bird's cage fell from its hook in the kitchen on two occasions without doing injury to the bird. There was no way, as far as the Wattersons could see, for the cage to have slipped from its hanging, but it did. To insure that the cage would not fall again, Watterson sharpened the angle of the hook which held it.

Despite the precaution, the family returned home one day to find the cage had fallen, and the canary had escaped and had drowned in the aquarium in the family room.

There was also the time, they recall, when four large lithographs of Civil War scenes fell from the wall in the family room. Each picture had been affixed securely and separately to the wall, but they all fell simultaneously. And not a glass was broken or a frame scratched.

"There was nobody in that part of the house when the lithographs fell," Watterson says. "Nobody around anywhere. I can't explain it unless Tobe's or Olin's pacing jarred the pictures loose.

"Was it Tobe or was it Olin? I wonder...."

79

The Ghosts Of The
Thirteen Patriots

"We will hang thirteen of the prisoners, one for each of the rebellious colonies," Colonel Thomas Browne ordered. "The hangings," he continued, "will be done right here in the stairwell of the trading house where I can watch the show."

It was September 18, 1780, and Colonel Browne was getting cruel vengeance for the rough treatment he had received at the hands of Augusta patriots five years earlier.

He did not know that his cold-blooded orders would be responsible for making the trading house, Mackay's Trading House, the "most haunted house in America." Here at the Mackay House, 1822 Broad Street, Augusta, are the ghosts of the thirteen martyred patriots and, most pathetic of all, the ghost of the grieving mother whose two young sons were executed by Colonel Browne that gory day.

The story of the patriots and their ghosts is entwined in the history of Georgia's role in the American Revolution. The story began in the summer of 1775 when Thomas Browne was living in Augusta. There were many Loyalists in Georgia at that time for Georgia, unlike other colonies, had a royal governor (James Wright) who was well-liked and

81

respected and under whose leadership Georgia had prospered.

Browne was among the group of staunch Loyalists. He was probably more outspoken in his support of King George III than other Augusta Loyalists, and he reportedly denounced the Liberty Boys, who were calling for rebellion, quite openly.

His words angered the Liberty Boys, and they demonstrated their displeasure by capturing Browne, pouring hot tar over him, and then emptying the contents of feather pillows onto the sticky tar.

With their prisoner tarred and feathered, they hoisted him to the seat of a mule-drawn wagon and paraded him through the streets of downtown Augusta. The conveyance was appropriately decorated with signs, and heralds trotted along beside the mules to announce the name of the wagon's passenger (many of Browne's acquaintances would not have recognized him otherwise) and to proclaim his crimes.

At the end of his humiliating ride, the Liberty Boys ordered Browne to leave Georgia within twenty-four hours. It did not take Browne nearly that long to depart from Augusta. His servant helped him scrub and scrape his coating of tar and feathers—or most of it—off, and he left Georgia for South Carolina.

Browne swore to get vengeance for the treatment he had received in Augusta, and he warned, "You citizens of Augusta will pay dearly for the indignity and suffering you inflicted upon me!"

Soon after his forced removal to South Carolina, Browne offered his services to the Crown and was made a lieutenant colonel in the British Army. Browne had a distinguished military record as a British officer by the time Augusta fell to the British in 1780.

General Archibald Campbell had little trouble taking Augusta when he marched two thousand of His Majesty's troops toward that city. The American officer in charge of Augusta's defense, Colonel Andrew Williamson, appeared to believe that the British were on the verge of winning the war, so he made only token resistance. His name later appeared on the roster of British officers.

For two weeks after the surrender of Augusta, Colonel Campbell terrorized the countryside, burning, hanging, looting, destroying. The victims of his ruthless tyranny prayed that Campbell would be replaced. They would have curbed or amended their prayers had they known that Campbell's replacement would be Thomas Browne, Colonel Thomas Browne of the British Army.

So Colonel Browne was back in Augusta as military commander of the city that had disgraced and dishonored him, and he gloated over his triumphant return. The laughter and the ridicule of the crowds when he had been made an ignominious public spectacle still echoed in his memory, and he determined to give Augusta no cause for laughter, not ever again.

Colonel Browne immediately began a systematic campaign of physical punishment, destruction of property, arrests, and harrassments designed to break the spirits of the Patriots.

Meantime, not far from Augusta, General Elijah Clarke was training American militia, three hundred men, for a surprise assault on Augusta. He wanted to win control of the city from Browne, whom he hated. General Clarke and his men moved toward Augusta on September 14, 1780. They focused their attack on Mackay's Trading House, a large three-story frame building a mile and a half west of town.

Several Indians who were allies of the British and a company of King's Rangers commanded by Captain Andrew Johnson were inside the trading house when the Patriots approached. They were soon reinforced by soldiers under the command of Colonel Browne.

The house where the patriots were hanged is one of the state's historic sites.

General Clarke's troops surrounded the trading house and began a siege that was to last until September 18. The upper stories of the structure provided excellent vantage points for the Tory sharpshooters. They, from that height, had an almost unobstructed view of the activities of the attackers and could shoot down any Patriots who moved within range of their guns.

Although the British sympathizers inside the trading house had a strategic military advantage over General Clarke's forces, they did have serious problems: there was no supply of food nor was there any water in the building. Medical supplies were lacking, too, and there was nothing to ease the suffering of wounded men.

September can be hot in Georgia, very hot, and the heat of those waning summer days made the thirst of the men trapped inside the building almost unbearable. By the fourth day, heat, thirst, hunger, and pain had driven some of the defenders almost mad.

The cries for water and pleas for medical attention (casualties were heavy on both sides) were overheard with satisfaction by General Clarke's men who reckoned that their enemies would soon surrender. Their reckoning was wrong, for they forgot to consider the tough, stubborn character of Colonel Browne.

"There will be no surrender. We will continue to fight," Colonel Browne told his men.

After that pronouncement, he refused to be influenced by the sounds of his troops' pleadings or by the sights of their sufferings. He cursed the circumstances that had brought about his being trapped in a building without provisions, and he denounced the operator of the trading post for not having a proper stock of goods in the establishment. He forgot, perhaps, that his own policies of permitting troops to confiscate private property could have been partly responsible for the bare shelves and empty boxes.

There was a brief period of hope for relief when one of Colonel Browne's men found several large bundles in one of the building's storerooms. But when the wrappings were torn away and the contents spilled out on the floor, there was nothing but gimcracks intended for Indian trade: glass beads, mirrors, knives, cloth, combs.

Colonel Browne cursed again and kicked the pile of baubles, scattering the cheap items across the room. He did not notice, nor would he have cared, that his boot heel shattered one of the mirrors.

It was soon after this episode that Colonel Browne was seriously wounded. Bullets from the Patriots' guns inflicted deep and painful wounds in both thighs. His injuries further infuriated Colonel Browne. "The scoundrels! The blasted scoundrels! How dare they shoot me?" he thundered.

He bound his wounds tightly to staunch the bleeding, and then he ordered two of his men to lift him to a chair near a window where he could continue to fire at his adversaries.

On the fifth day of the siege, British reinforcements and friendly Cherokee Indians came to the rescue of Colonel Browne and his men. Their arrival made it expedient for General Clarke's troops to retreat. As they began their hasty withdrawal, the Patriots realized they would have to leave behind twenty-eight men who were so badly wounded that they could not be moved from the field.

Another man—a boy, really, for he was only fifteen—chose to remain with his wounded older brother.

"Come on, Glass! Hurry! We must get away before our escape route is cut off!" General Clarke urged the youth.

"Sir, I cannot leave my brother," the boy replied. "I can't. It wouldn't be right. I can't leave him."

The wounded brother—he was seventeen—also pled with the boy soldier to go, but he would not. The boy was kneeling beside his brother, comforting and encouraging him, when Colonel Browne's soldiers snatched him to his feet and hurried him off to the trading house.

And so it was that the two Glass brothers who had grown up together on the Georgia frontier, had hunted deer and had trapped rabbits together, had swum together in Little River, had cleared fields and planted crops together, and had joined up with General Clarke's guerrillas together died together that September day in Augusta.

General Clarke had assumed that the wounded men would be treated as prisoners of war, but again this assumption failed to evaluate correctly Colonel Browne's character.

"These men are not prisoners of war. They are traitors," the Tory commander decreed. "And they will be dealt with accordingly."

He looked closely at each of the twenty-nine prisoners, hoping to find among their number some who had participated in tarring and feathering him in Augusta five years earlier, but he saw no familiar faces. Perhaps he was disappointed, but he quickly gave his attention to the details of the executions.

The trading house was of unusual construction with an open-air stairway rising in a spiral from the back porch to the upper stories. It was this stairwell which Colonel Browne chose as the site for the hangings.

His men installed a stout hook at the top of the stairwell, and through this hook was run the rope, the hangman's rope.

Colonel Browne had been moved to a bed in a rear bedroom on the lower floor. Now he had the bed shifted and propped himself up on pillows so that he could have a clear view of the bodies as they dangled from the rope in the stairwell.

One by one the prisoners walked or were carried (some of them were too badly wounded to walk) up the stairway to

The trading house had an open-air stairway rising from the back porch.

where the noose waited. And one by one they dropped to their deaths: Ashby, Duke, Burgamy, Redding, Richetson, Darling, W. Willey, R. Willey, the Glass brothers, and three men whose names were not recorded.

Colonel Browne's gaze never veered from the dreadful scene.

He did not watch, however, when the remaining sixteen prisoners were turned over to the Indians to be tortured to death. Indian torture was too inhumanly cruel for even the cold-hearted Colonel Browne to enjoy.

A report of the hangings was made to Lord George Germain, King George III's minister, by the Royal Governor of Georgia, James Wright, who wrote,

"Thirteen of the Prisoners who broke their Paroles and came against Augusta have been hang'd which I hope will have a very Good Effect.

"Several Plantations or Settlements on the Ceded Lands belonging to those who were at Augusta have been Burnt and Laid Waste."

The house where the Patriots were hanged is now one of the state's historic sites administered by the Georgia Historical Commission. Hundreds of visitors go there each year to see the stairwell which served as a gallows that September day in 1780.

Some of the visitors stand in the stairwell, close their eyes, and count to thirteen, slowly. Then they hear, they say, the thud of Patriots dropping to their deaths.

Other visitors stand on the thirteenth step for it is here that scores of people have heard the moans of the condemned men.

The pathetic ghost of Mrs. Glass, mother of the teen-age brothers, is never heard at Mackay House, but several residents of the place have seen her. Mrs. Glass, the story goes, died of a broken heart when she learned of her sons' deaths. She had tried to keep her boys at home, had tried to convince them that they were too young to go off to war, for she had a premonition that they would not return.

Friends tried to shield her from learning of the brutal manner in which her sons were killed, but thoughtless gossips told her the complete details of the hangings. The shock and grief were more than she could bear, and she prayed constantly that death would take her, too.

Now her spirit is seen most often on the third floor of Mackay House, the figure of a thin woman moving slowly around the room as though she were searching for someone dear to her. She has been seen, too, this ghostly figure, coming down the winding stairs to the back porch where she pauses and holds out her hands in supplication to an invisible presence in the rear bedroom, the bedroom where Colonel Thomas Browne lay as he watched thirteen brave men die.

The Light In
The Graveyard

St. Simons Island is so rich in ghost lore that natives there seldom agree on which of the many supernatural happenings is the most outstanding.

Some of the islanders favor the story of Mary the Wanderer (or Mary de Wanda), the grieving woman who meanders along deserted roadways searching for her drowned lover.

Other residents of St. Simons like best the ghost of a lightkeeper who for years haunted the tall white lighthouse on the tip of the island. His heavy footsteps on the spiral stairway were familiar sounds to the men working in the tower, and their families who lived in the cottage adjoining the lighthouse accepted the clatter of the restless feet as a natural supplement to their household noises.

Then there are the stories of the shipload of captives from the African Ibo tribe who walked into the sea rather than spend their lives in slavery and whose doleful chant, "The water brought us, the water will take us away," is still heard around the mouth of Dunbar Creek, and of Flora de Cookpot whose delectable, calorie-filled foods can be smelled

The lightkeepers' heavy footsteps still echo on the spiral stairway.

simmering on an invisible stove, and of the tormented ghost of a former owner of Kelvyn Grove Plantation who roams the grounds seeking his murderer.

But the most often told and certainly the most appealing ghost story on the island is the account of the light in the graveyard at Christ Church, Frederika.

Nobody remembers her full name, but all residents of St. Simons know the story of the young woman whose fear of the dark prompted her husband, after her death, to put a lighted candle on her grave each night for as long as he lived.

According to the story, Emma, on whose grave the candle glows, had always been afraid of the dark. Her mother traced the fear back to an old nurse who whispered terrifying tales of witches and vampires and voodoo and evil spirits to the child "to make her behave." The nurse was assigned other, and decidedly less pleasant, duties when it became known that she was deliberately frightening Emma, but by then the damage had been done.

Emma's father, who loved his only daughter deeply and who usually indulged her every whim, took her fears lightly at first.

"There's nothing to be afraid of," he assured her. "Forget all those false tales. Nothing is going to hurt you. Not ever."

Though reason and reassurance seemed to be effective in dealing with the child's fears in the daytime, when night came the dread of the dark possessed her again. She screamed in fright if she was left alone in the dark for even a few minutes.

Her mother tried to soothe Emma by reminding her of God's care and by teaching her a poem about the dark which began,

"The dark is soft and gentle.
The dark is kind and sweet.
The dark will pat my pillow
And love me as I sleep."
Neither the reminder nor the poetry was effective.

Then Emma's father lost patience with what he termed her "senseless, spoiled display of fear."

"Put Emma to bed as usual," he instructed her new nurse. "Make sure she is comfortable, and then put out the lamp, close the door, and leave her alone. She is quite old enough to remain in a darkened room by herself, and she must not be indulged in this childishness any longer!"

The nurse reluctantly did as she was told, but as soon as

she had put out the lamp and closed the door, she hurried from the house and walked down a winding plantation road for nearly half a mile until she could no longer hear Emma's screams.

Emma's father steeled himself against entering her room, and he forbade any other member of the household to respond to her pleas for light. Finally though it was her father himself who went in to her. He had intended to be firm and to order her to stop creating such a furor, but when he saw that she was hysterical with fear, and when she collapsed in his arms, he gently placed her in bed, lighted a candle, and lay beside her until she fell asleep. He left the candle burning by her bed when he tiptoed from the room.

The next day he retracted the orders he had given the nurse, and he instructed her never to leave Emma alone in the dark but to make sure that a lighted candle, a fresh candle each night, was left beside her bed.

Even then her parents believed that in time Emma would outgrow her fear of the dark, but as the years passed the young girl became increasingly dependent on the security which the burning candle gave her.

She developed a distressing anxiety about running out of candles, and she began hoarding stubs which she collected from candlesticks around the house. She hid the stubs in her bureau drawer until her mother discovered them and was about to throw them away (one of them had melted and had matted the lace and tatting on a nearly new chemise). Emma begged so pitifully to be allowed to keep the pieces of candles that her mother agreed to let her put them in a box in the corner of the pantry.

Except for this fear of the dark, Emma was a normal, happy, attractive girl. She had many friends, and her invitations to parties and to outings kept her social calendar filled. When they were younger, her friends sometimes teased her about being afraid of the dark, but in time they accepted it as being as natural as the fears some of them had of snakes or of water or even of horses. A few of the girls even considered Emma's nightly candle a bit romantic and wished that their parents would allow them to cultivate such a dramatic idiosyncrasy.

As for the boys, knowledge of Emma's fear of darkness aroused their protective instincts, and she was never lacking for escorts dedicated to guarding her from whatever dangers might lurk in the shadows.

It was at a houseparty in Brunswick that Emma met the young man, Phillip, whom she was later to marry. He had recently moved to Brunswick from the Carolinas to join a cotton brokerage firm, so he knew nothing of Emma's terror of darkness.

He only knew that he loved her.

Emma, of course, was aware of Phillip's love, but she did not feel that she could or should encourage it until he knew about her abnormal reaction to darkness. Yet she could not bring herself to tell him about it. For the first time in her life Emma was truly embarrassed to talk of her fear. It seemed so childish, so beneath the dignity of a woman old enough to be thinking of marriage. Night after night she worried about telling him of her "affliction," staying awake until her candle burned low in its holder.

On the night, several months after they had met, that Phillip asked her to become his wife, she knew she could no longer delay the revelation.

"There is something I must tell you," she began. Already her voice was shaking and she was near tears. "I cannot accept your proposal of marriage—I do love you, Phillip—until I am completely honest with you about my background. You see—"

Phillip was stunned. What did she have in her past that

95

would upset her so? Had there been an unfortunate love affair? Did she have a dread malady? Surely she was not in love with someone else!

"What is it, Emma? What is it? Tell me. Nothing can change my love for you. Nothing!"

"It's—oh, Phillip, I'm afraid of the dark!" Emma blurted out.

"Afraid of the dark! Is that all?" Phillip laughed with relief.

"Don't laugh, Phillip. Please don't. It's awful, this fear of mine." The tears came.

Phillip wiped her eyes with his handkerchief, and then cupping her hands in his, he said, "Emma, you must not cry. And you must not be afraid. Not ever. Not of anything. I will take care of you. Always."

They were married, Emma and Phillip, at Christ Church, Frederika, and afterwards they stood in the shade of the massive oaks outside the church, the same oaks beneath which Charles and John Wesley had preached more than a century before, to receive the good wishes of their friends.

Phillip had taken Emma's confession of her fear of the dark rather lightly, but in time he learned to sleep quite well with a candle burning all night in their bedroom. Except for this adjustment, Emma and Phillip were completely happy together. They moved, after several months, from Brunswick to Frederika on St. Simons Island where Phillip helped his father-in-law with managing his plantation and his shipping interests.

It was not long after this move that Phillip observed that Emma was becoming overly concerned about her supply of candles. She went to her childhood home and got the old box of candle stubs from the pantry, melted them down, and made new candles.

Then she busied herself making candles of beeswax. She

explained to Phillip that the candles of beeswax burned more evenly and cast a more pleasant light than did candles molded of tallow.

By this time Emma had learned to estimate with amazing accuracy how long a candle would burn, and she made her candles different lengths to conform with the difference in the lengths of the nights. For example, candles intended for use in June were shorter than those to be used in December since June nights are shorter than December nights. She separated her candles by lengths, wrapped them in bundles, and labeled each bundle with the name of the month in which the candles were to be used. She then stored them in a cool basement closet.

She spent more and more time making candles, though she never let her candle-making interfere with her household duties or with her service to the church (she provided candles, taking them from her own precious store, for use in the sanctuary each Sunday, and she also taught a Sunday School class and was a leader in missionary work).

When Phillip, with the utmost patience, pointed out to Emma that she had enough candles to last for several years, and when he suggested that she devote her time to other, more pleasant activities, she replied,

"But the dark is so dreadful. I cannot bear it if I do not have the security of knowing I have many candles to protect me. Please understand, Phillip."

Though he did not really understand, Phillip humored her and continued to provide her with the growing amounts of wax and wicks she required. He loved her very much, and his concern for her obsession with candle-making only deepened that love.

Emma was making candles one afternoon when she spilled some of the hot wax on her arm, inflicting a deep and painful burn. She used the usual home remedies, but the injury did

97

not heal properly. Infection set in and, despite the best efforts of doctors brought in by Phillip, blood poisoning developed.

Less than a week after the accident, Emma died.

She had realized the seriousness of her condition, and she talked calmly of death. "I am quite ready to die if it is God's will," she told the rector when he came to visit her.

But to Phillip she said,

"It will be so dark, so very dark—"

Phillip leaned close to her and whispered, "You'll always have a light. Always."

After the funeral, in the late twilight of that long day, Phillip got a candle from the supply Emma had made and walked to her grave beside Christ Church. He pushed the candle into the soft dirt and lighted it.

"Here's your candle, my darling," he said. Then he turned quickly and went back to his empty house.

Every night for as long as he lived Phillip made this solitary trek to the graveyard to place a candle on Emma's grave. When the weather was rainy or windy, he put the candle inside a small lantern fashioned of glass and tin so that the flame would not go out, but the weather was never too bad nor was business ever too pressing to prevent his performance of this nightly ritual.

Neighbors remarked on his faithfulness, and they explained the significance of the burning candle to strangers who inquired.

When Phillip died, he was buried beside Emma at Christ Church.

For several nights after Phillip's death, people passing the graveyard saw the familiar light on Emma's grave. They were surprised at first, but they decided that some of the neighbors were carrying on Phillip's custom of placing a candle there.

However, inquiry disclosed that no one on the island was responsible for the light, no one was taking candles to the grave. The source of the burning taper was—and still is—a

Here at Christ Church Cemetery the lonely candle glowed.

mystery.

In the years that have followed, hundreds of people on St. Simons have seen the patch of light like the soft glow of a candle on a time-weathered grave at Christ Church.

The brick wall around the church property hides the graves from the road now so that the light is not seen by motorists driving past the burial spot. However, people who walk down the road beneath the moss-hung limbs of the old oaks or who pause to lean against the brick wall and stare at the graves still tell occasionally of seeing a peculiar, flickering light.

These sightings prompt the re-telling of the story of the young woman who was afraid of the dark and of her devoted husband who promised,

"You'll always have a light. Always."

The Ghost Who Moved With His House

Nobody now is quite sure when it was that the ghost of Colonel George W. Fish first came storming back to his earthly home.

Some people say the Colonel made his presence known in his house in Oglethorpe soon after his murder in 1871 and that he was surely present in the courthouse there when the murderers were brought to trial. Others say it was some years before his restless spirit returned to Oglethorpe.

Mr. and Mrs. Donald Nelson, who now live in Atlanta, know that Colonel Fish's spirit was quite active in the house he once owned when they moved it from Oglethorpe to Americus in 1969. Mr. Nelson even had a pleasant—if unexpected—conversation with the ghost.

Colonel Fish's story, or this part of it, begins in 1852 after he had moved to Oglethorpe from nearby Pulaski County. He bought a large lot on Randolph Street, and on this lot he built a house.

His house was not the traditional Greek Revival style so popular in the South at that time but was patterned after the houses of wealthy British planters in the West Indies. It had

101

two levels, a raised basement of handmade bricks and a frame upper level where the family moved each summer to "escape the vapors." Two bannistered flights of steps rose from the front to the second floor portico, the main entrance to the house.

Colonel Fish was a scholarly man, though not stuffily so, who read a great deal. His love of reading and his attendant desire to have good light probably account for the large windows on the second level of the house: each of them measures five by nine feet and has 24 panes.

It is beside one of these windows in the front parlor, where a comfortable chair and volumes of Shakespeare would surely be to the Colonel's liking, that the present owners of the house, Dr. and Mrs. Gatewood Dudley, most often feel Colonel Fish's presence. So aware are they of an unseen visitor in this room that they call the chair, a barrel chair upholstered in red velvet, "Colonel Fish's chair," and they reserve it almost exclusively for his use. Few mortals feel completely comfortable sitting in it.

When Colonel Fish completed his house, he and his wife planned the landscaping of the spacious grounds. He had camellia bushes imported from France for her pleasure, and these bushes are said to be the parent plants of camellias which flourish throughout the area today.

The Colonel, who was also known as Judge Fish—nobody is sure which title he preferred—did not spend all his time supervising the building of his house and the planting of his gardens. He was a prominent attorney, and his thriving law practice kept him busy in the county seat town of Oglethorpe. At that time Oglethorpe had a population of about 16,000 and was one of the major cities in Georgia. In fact, it was almost chosen as capital of the state.

Colonel Fish, it is recorded, was a genial host who delighted in entertaining newspaper editors, legislators,

*It is near this comfortable chair in the front parlor that
Colonel Fish's presence is often felt.*

lawyers, and planters at his home on Randolph Street. He
provided his guests with the finest wines and brandies, and at
dinner he served choice champagne from his cellar stock. His
home was a social center particularly during court week when
men from throughout the county converged on Oglethorpe
to settle legal matters or to observe court proceedings.

His law business and his social nature combined to
encourage his making rather frequent trips to Americus and
to Macon. Friends who sometimes accompanied him on these
trips reported that it was Colonel Fish's habit upon arriving
at the city (they always made the trip by train) to purchase a
return ticket to Oglethorpe before leaving the depot.

"I want to be prepared for any eventuality," Colonel Fish
would explain. He had seen too many men stranded penniless
in a large city after an unlucky turn of a card, and he had no
wish for such an experience to befall him.

However, Colonel Fish was totally unprepared for the eventuality awaiting him the tragic night he returned from a business trip to Macon. Lurking in the shadows at the courthouse in Oglethorpe that night was John Holsenback who shot and killed Colonel Fish as the attorney walked from the depot toward his home. Certainly Colonel Fish, with all his planning, never imagined that he would be ambushed and fatally shot with his own gun. But he was.

The exact episode which incited the murder is uncertain, but it seems that Colonel Fish had offended John Holsenback in some fashion, and Holsenback swore to get revenge. Holsenback's bitter anger was encouraged by his close friend, Jim Loyd. Some residents said Loyd hated Colonel Fish, too, because of "undue attention" he felt the Colonel showed Mrs. Loyd. In any event, Holsenback and Loyd, their bond of friendship tightened by their common hatred of Colonel Fish, began to devise a plot for destroying him.

"The only thing to do is to kill him," Loyd reportedly said. And Holsenback agreed.

The morning they saw Colonel Fish walk alone to the depot and board the train to Macon, the two men put their murder plan into action. They had decided that shooting Colonel Fish would be the most satisfactory method of disposing of him and also the method least likely to result in their apprehension. The choice of a gun presented a problem. Or it did until Loyd suggested that they use the intended victim's own gun to fire the fatal shot.

Loyd was a gun expert of sorts, and he often hung around the gun shop in downtown Oglethorpe. He had noticed that Colonel Fish had brought one of his favorite weapons to the shop to be repaired, and he had also noticed that, though the repairs had been made, Colonel Fish had not come to pick up the gun. So Loyd went to the shop and used such powers of persuasion that the repairman let him borrow Colonel Fish's

The old courthouse is a drug store now.

gun to shoot some squirrels.

"Don't worry," Loyd assured the repairman, "I'll have this gun back in your shop before Colonel Fish ever needs it." He laughed in a way the repairman did not quite understand.

Loyd prepared a proper wadding for the gun and turned it over to Holsenback who was to do the actual shooting.

When Holsenback heard the train arrive at the depot late that night, he and the gun were waiting in the recessed entryway of the old courthouse. (The building still stands, and a drug store is housed in it now.) After a few minutes Holsenback heard footsteps approaching from the direction of the depot, and he peeped from his hiding place. He saw Colonel Fish walking rapidly toward the courthouse, followed by his servant who had met the train and was carrying his master's heavy briefcase.

The downtown streets were deserted and dark, but the moving silhouette of his victim presented Holsenback with an excellent target. He waited, impatient and a bit nervous now, until Colonel Fish was well within range. Then he aimed and fired.

Colonel Fish slumped to the sidewalk, mortally wounded.

The terrified servant fled from the scene.

Holsenback slipped away from his ambush unnoticed.

It was not until early the next morning that Colonel Fish's body was discovered. The servant, sole witness to the murder, had been too frightened to tell anyone what had happened. Since Colonel Fish sometimes found it necessary to spend the night in Macon on his business trips there, Mrs. Fish was not worried when he failed to return on schedule, and she did not report his absence from home. And though several residents said later that they had heard the noise of the gun being fired, they had paid it little attention.

News of the murder spread rapidly, and a large crowd gathered at the scene. In the crowd was John Holsenback. He listened as the coroner ruled that Colonel George W. Fish had been murdered by an unknown assailant, and he joined in the outraged denounciation of the killer.

Holsenback had a reputation for helpfulness, for being willing to lend a hand when needed, so it seemed natural when he offered to help move the body to the Fish home. At the home he helped the undertaker place the body in the coffin, performing the task with amazing tenderness, and he spoke proper words of sympathy and comfort to the grieving widow.

The coffin was placed in the wide hall on the upper level of the house, and it was here that lines of friends filed past to pay their last respects to the deceased. Holsenback remained at the house for some time. He spoke quietly, using tones fitting the occasion, with groups of visitors about "this terrible, sad thing which has happened to this fine man" before he departed to meet Loyd and give his accomplice a full report of the murder and the subsequent events.

Once the funeral was over (Holsenback was not asked to be a pallbearer though he doubtless would have been willing to serve), the attention of Oglethorpe and much of the rest of Georgia centered on apprehending the murderer. Colonel Fish had been prominent in legal, political, and social life, and his friends throughout the state demanded that his cowardly murderer be found and brought to justice immediately.

Governor Rufus Bullock, a friend of Fish, dispatched two detectives to Oglethorpe to work on the case. The detectives, named Rasberry and Murphy, were suspicious of Holsenback from the first, but they had no evidence against him.

One day Murphy, who was a very fat man, entered a shop where Holsenback was standing. Murphy picked up a woven fish basket, held it in front of his face, and peeped through the slits right into the eyes of John Holsenback.

"You are the guilty man," Murphy said slowly, still staring at Holsenback through the fish basket.

Murphy's bold accusation and his dramatic use of the symbolic fish basket shocked and frightened Holsenback so deeply that he made an oral confession on the spot. He was arrested and so was his friend Jim Loyd.

The two detectives needed more evidence against Holsenback and Loyd, so they devised a scheme to hide in the men's jail cell and listen to their conversations, a sort of early version of present-day wiretapping. Before the prisoners were brought to their cell, the detectives got inside a large box which was then disguised as a washstand. Just as the detectives had hoped, Loyd and Holsenback, thinking they were alone and that no one could overhear their conversation, talked freely about the murder.

At one point Loyd declared, "This is hell," to which his friend replied, "No, but it's on the road to hell."

Rasberry and Murphy had planned that when they overheard all they needed to know about the murder, they would burst from the box and confront the guilty men. So when that point in their eavesdropping was reached, Rasberry gave the signal and the detectives sprang from hiding. At least Rasberry did. Murphy was too fat to get through the opening, and assistance had to be summoned to disentangle him and pull him out.

Despite this unexpected complication, the ruse had worked, and the detectives had gathered enough information to bring murder charges against Holsenback and Loyd.

Some people, even this soon after Colonel Fish's death, said that they were aware of his ghostly presence around the jail and at the courthouse.

"He would have delighted in seeing the fat detective caught in that box—what a tale he would have made of it!" they said.

"And there's almost nothing he enjoyed more than a good murder trial," they added, "so it's just natural that his spirit would be hovering around the courthouse."

The trial was held in the Macon County courthouse, the very building whose shadow touched the spot where Colonel Fish had been slain. Holsenback and Loyd were found guilty and were sentenced to be hanged.

Lawyers for the condemned men asked for a new trial, contending that many factors prevented their having a fair trial in Oglethorpe. While they waited in jail for action on this request, Loyd paced back and forth in his cell so constantly that he wore the heads of the nails in the flooring slick. Holsenback was busier: he carefully removed a section of bricks from his cell wall. Then he made a rope from a blanket and slid to freedom. However, since he was slightly crippled, he could not run fast so he was promptly taken into custody again.

Members of Loyd's family went to Milledgeville to plead with Governor James Smith, who had recently taken office, to pardon Loyd, but the governor refused to intervene in the case.

On the day of the hangings, people came from all around Oglethorpe to watch the event.

When the condemned men were brought to the gallows, Holsenback was penitent and begged for forgiveness, but

Loyd remained defiant to the end. He lounged on the wooden steps leading up to the platform, and he spat tobacco juice on his waiting coffin.

"Bury me north and south," he instructed. "I've always been crossways with the world, and I might as well be buried that way." He was.

Also according to his request, Loyd was buried wearing a buttonless undershirt with a sheet wrapped around his body.

The attitudes of the men's wives differed, too. Mrs. Holsenback, who had separated from her husband some time before, entered into the carnival spirit of the occasion and referred to his hanging as a "gander stretching." Mrs. Loyd, on the other hand, marched up and down the road beseeching God to send down a curse that would open the earth and swallow Macon County.

What a spectacle that must have been for Colonel Fish's ghost if, as some people contended, he was present for the occasion!

It has been more than a hundred years since Colonel Fish was murdered and his killers were hanged, but tales about those events are still told and retold in Macon County, particularly when there are reports that Colonel Fish's ghost has been active. For the Colonel's spirit has never been completely peaceful. Through the years occupants of his Oglethorpe home have told of hearing his footsteps walk across the floor, and they have told of overhearing loud arguments between Colonel Fish and his wife, both long dead.

Mr. and Mrs. Nelson heard some of these stories when they bought the old Fish home and prepared to move it from Oglethorpe to Americus. Few lawyers believe in ghosts, however, so Nelson listened to the stories, smiled, and went placidly ahead with his plans to transplant the old house.

Then several strange things happened. Carpenters hired to

prepare the foundations for the house in Americus were to do most of their work at night, but something kept interfering with them. Neat piles of sand were scattered and strewn about by an invisible intruder. Mortar boxes mysteriously overturned. Tools disappeared. The workers became so upset (some of them were downright scared) that all night work had to be cancelled. In fact, before the move was complete, the Nelsons had two complete crews of workmen walk off the job.

Mr. Nelson recalls that during the move itself everything possible went wrong: windows broke for no reason; the house creaked and popped as though warning of impending disintegration; and the rig with the house on it slid off the road and into a ditch with no apparent cause.

A picture taken by Mr. Nelson while the house was being prepared for the move shows a strange image, an eerie smear which is not a smear at all but could be the ghost of Colonel Fish. Mr. Nelson is not sure.

He is sure though that he had a conversation with the ghost of Colonel Fish soon after the house was set on its new foundations in Americus. As Mr. Nelson tells it, he was sitting before the fire in the den one night, resting a bit after a strenuous day, when he glanced around and saw a slender, dark-haired stranger standing beside him. The visitor seemed to be quite at home, as indeed he was.

Mr. Nelson realized immediately that his guest was Colonel Fish, and the two lawyers had a pleasant conversation. Colonel Fish admitted that he had been upset over having his house moved, that he did not understand why his familiar living quarters should be uprooted and transported to a strange setting, but he was no longer hostile.

"He told me he was happy with the way things had gone," Mr. Nelson recalls, "and he even was apologetic about the trouble he had caused.

"I was not frightened or upset by Colonel Fish's visit because it seemed so natural. It was almost as though an old friend, someone I knew well, had come to visit. We had a leisurely, relaxed conversation for perhaps ten or fifteen minutes."

During that conversation Mr. Nelson thanked the Colonel for his approval of the Nelsons' restoration of his home, and in a gesture of Southern hospitality he assured Colonel Fish that he would find a friendly welcome in the Nelson household any time he chose to visit.

After this exchange of pleasantries, the apparition disappeared, and Mr. Nelson hastened from the room to tell his wife about his strange visitor. Later he gave full details of the visit to Dr. and Mrs. Gatewood Dudley when they bought the house and moved into it in 1971.

So when Colonel Fish returns to visit his old home now, he comes not to harrass or to argue or to create a commotion but to admire the restored beauty of a place he loved.

Colonel Fish's house was patterned after the houses of British planters.

The Strange Blue Goose

It was an unusual mission that brought Mrs. Jubal Frances Aline White and her husband all the way from their Texas home to the little Georgia town of Jeffersonville in the fall of 1969.

"I'm going to Georgia to look for a sea shell," Mrs. White told her neighbors in Arlington, Texas, before they left.

"A sea shell?" the neighbors asked. "Isn't that a long way to go to look for a shell? There are lots of shells along the beaches right here in Texas, you know."

"But this is a special shell," Mrs. White explained. "It has been on my great-grandfather's grave for more than a century, and now I want to find it and bring it back to Texas to put on his widow's grave.

"Maybe it is foolish," Mrs. White admitted, "but I want great-grandmother Missouri Whitehead to have the mourning conch on her grave now."

Mrs. White first heard the story of the mourning conch from her grandmother, Frances Whitehead Wente, who had watched Missouri Whitehead place the shell on her husband's grave back in Georgia. As a child Mrs. White wondered about the story, trying to decide whether the shell really did exist or whether it was another of those "once upon a time" tales that her grandmother told so well.

She remembered being taken to the cemetery at Hemphill, Texas, and having an adult in the family point out the grave of Missouri Loyless Whitehead.

"That's your great-grandmother's grave," an aunt—she could not remember which one—said. "She came from Georgia to Texas after the War Between the States. Her husband had died, you know. Seems sad, her being buried here and him back there in Georgia. Right sad."

"Yes," another relative agreed, "but don't forget that he has the shell. It keeps him company, you might say."

"I'd hate to have to depend on a shell for company!" someone else in the group said. "But then if you're dead, I don't suppose it matters."

"Grandmother Whitehead thought it mattered," the aunt retorted. "That's why she left the shell, and that's why she talked about it for as long as she lived."

So the story was true, there really was a shell, a mourning conch, on a grave somewhere in Georgia, the child, Aline, decided.

Aline moved away from her bickering relatives and strolled over to look at a stone angel, a baby angel with a short robe and stiff curly hair and heavy wings.

"Aline! Don't step on the graves!" an aunt called after her.

So Aline carefully skirted each mound of earth and, though she was tempted, she took no shortcuts across the long stone slabs. She could not help thinking though how fine those smooth slabs would be for playing jacks or even for a game of hopscotch. The names and the dates carved on them would not interfere with the games, she thought, and she wondered if anybody ever played games in a graveyard.

After she had touched the wings of the stone angel,

running her stubby fingers along the rows of granite feathers, Aline looked at the other grave markers: lambs, tree trunks, flowers, statues of Jesus. She went to look closely at those which interested her, still being careful not to step on the graves.

Nowhere in the whole cemetery did Aline see a grave with a conch on it, not a single one.

The grown-ups were returning to their cars and were calling impatiently to Aline to hurry up. The child ran toward the road, and in her haste she stepped on the edge of a grave. Her foot sank through the crusty dirt and left the perfect print of her black patent leather shoe. Aline paused long enough to erase the print with the side of her shoe, stirring up a nest of ants as she did so.

Her path to the car led by her great-grandmother's grave, and as she ran past it Aline said softly,

"I'll get you a shell, Great-grandmother Missouri."

All the way home Aline thought about the shell. She closed her eyes so she could think hard, and the adults assumed she was asleep.

"The little thing's all tired out. Probably needs a tonic," one of the women commented.

Aline kept her eyes closed. She often pretended to be asleep for she had discovered that adults talked of very interesting subjects when they thought she was not listening.

This afternoon though Aline was too deep in her own thoughts to pay attention to the conversation of her relatives. She was trying to remember the story of the conch, every detail, just as her grandmother told it...

Charles and Missouri Whitehead were married in Georgia in the 1830s. The young couple set up housekeeping on a plantation in Twiggs County near the town of Marion. Marion has now vanished, as have other landmarks in the

115

area, but when Charles and Missouri lived nearby, Marion was a flourishing town.

It was in Marion that the Whiteheads bought the staple commodities they needed: sugar, coffee, wheat flour, and salt. Here, too, they frequently attended church services.

Macon, a real city, was not far away, but in those days a trip to Macon was a momentous event. Missouri had been to Macon on several occasions. Though she would have welcomed other trips there, she really wanted to go to Savannah.

Missouri had never seen the sea.

Charles had journeyed along the Georgia coast, and sometimes he would tell Missouri about the hypnotic sound of the waves hitting the shore and about how the water stretched on forever until it lost itself in the sky on the distant horizon. He told her, too, about the sea birds that flew low over the water and that patrolled the beach in search of food, and he described the shells that the waves deposited on the sands.

Once when he returned from a business trip to Savannah, Charles brought her a conch.

"Listen," he said, holding the big shell to her ear. "You can hear the sea roar. Listen."

"Is that how it sounds? Is it really?" Missouri asked delightedly. "If I close my eyes, I can pretend that I see the waves and the birds and the shells—"

At first Missouri used her shell as a doorstop in the parlor, as she had seen older ladies do, but the children were attracted to it, wanting to pick it up and listen to the sea roar, and she was afraid they would drop her treasure. Missouri put her shell up on .the mantel out of their reach. She turned the shell on its side so that the pale pink lining showed. Often as she passed through the room she paused to hold the shell close to her ear and hear its song.

The shell was still on the mantel years later when friends brought Charles' coffin into the room and placed it near the fireplace. It was 1853, and Charles was 43. He had been ill a long time.

One of the neighbors who came to sit up that night lifted the shell from the mantel, held it to his ear, and marveled at the sound of the sea. He passed it around the room to other friends who had come to share the vigil.

Missouri wanted to snatch the shell from them, wanted to shout, "That's mine! Mine and Charles'! Don't touch it!" But she knew they meant no harm, so she controlled her tongue, and when someone asked where the shell came from, she answered simply, "Mr. Whitehead brought it to me."

After her husband's death, Missouri ran their plantation alone. Her growing sons and the hands Charles had trained helped, of course, but Missouri was in charge. She always was.

Then came the War and the bitter time of Reconstruction.

One of Missouri's sons gave his life in the service of the Confederacy. His death was the family's greatest loss though their plantation was devastated, their slaves were gone, and their money was worthless.

"You don't grieve—you work," Missouri said when she talked about their losses. The truth was, she had never quit missing Charles, had never recovered from that loss.

Talk of Texas and the opportunities in the developing state interested Missouri, and she sent a son, Henry, to investigate.

"Come to Texas," Henry wrote back to Georgia to his mother. "Land is plentiful and it's so rich it will grow anything. And it's cheap."

So Missouri Whitehead sold her Georgia land, hid her money in a belt strapped around her tiny waist, and took her family to Texas.

It was difficult for Missouri to leave her home and her

117

friends in Georgia, but the hardest part was having to pay a final visit to her husband's grave. She knew she would never return. On that last visit, she took the shell, the conch Charles had given her, and placed it on his grave.

"Listen, Charles," she whispered, "and you will hear our shell singing a perpetual reminder of my grief and of my love."

She pushed the shell firmly into the dirt, and then she walked rapidly away. Somehow the act comforted her for she felt that Charles knew the shell was on his grave and that he understood and was less lonely.

It was this story that Aline Ragan (later to be Mrs. G. A. White) reviewed in her mind as she rode home from her great-grandmother's grave that afternoon, and it was this story which prompted her years later to look for the shell.

Her husband went with her to Georgia to help in the search. Though he understood her motivation and was quite sympathetic, he was not optimistic that the mission would be successful. He tried to prepare Mrs. White for possible disappointment by reminding her that they had only vague directions for locating her great-grandfather's grave. Even if they found the grave, he pointed out, the chance that the conch would still be where Missouri Whitehead had placed it more than a century before was small indeed.

For almost two days after they began their search for the grave site, it appeared that Mr. White's predictions were correct. Although they inquired of local residents in Twiggs County, checked records, and rode hundreds of miles on rural roads, they did not find the private cemetery in which Charles Whitehead was buried.

Then, late in the afternoon of the second day, October 12, Mr. and Mrs. White found the burying place. It was in a field near the road, not far from Bullard. A rusty iron fence with sharp pickets separated the graves, perhaps a dozen of them,

118

Cemetery where Charles Whitehead is buried.

from the cultivated acres, and a decaying oak tree shaded them. Though it was almost mid-October, there had not been a killing frost, and the graves were covered with a tangle of vines and weeds.

The couple pulled the iron gate open and entered the enclosure. They could see the inscriptions on some of the markers, and none of them bore the name they sought.

"Perhaps it was too much to hope that we could find the shell after all these years," Mrs. White said, but her husband was too busy pushing aside vines and tramping down weeds to hear her.

Then they saw it, the spiked crown of a weathered conch protruding from the Georgia earth.

Neither of them spoke for a second. Then Mrs. White exclaimed, "That's it! The shell—it's really here!" She stooped and reached for it and then drew her hands back.

"No," she said, "let's not disturb it now. We will leave it right here until tomorrow. Then we'll bring someone with us to verify our find."

Next day, October 13, Mrs. White went into Macon to do some historical and genealogical research, leaving Mr. White to go for the shell in the company of Hugh Lawson Faulk of Dry Branch, Georgia, and a Mr. Sanders who was a neighbor of Mr. Faulk. With them was the Faulks' hired man, Lewis Williams.

First the men assured themselves that the shell was still there. Then they cleared away the vegetation and the debris from the cemetery, a chore they had promised Mrs. White they would perform.

Lewis Williams was leaning over to lift the shell from the grave when Sanders asked,

"Where did that strange-looking goose come from?"

Walking along the side of the fence and pecking in the grass growing there was a big blue goose. The bird seemed to be quite at ease, not at all perturbed by the presence of the four men. It actually seemed to be watching what the four of them were doing.

"Where did it come from?" one of the men asked. "It

120

wasn't here when we came, and none of us saw it come. That's strange."

"I don't know where it came from, but I do know that I never saw a goose like it before," Faulk said. "I've lived around here about all my life, but there has never been a bird like that here."

"Maybe I can catch him," Williams volunteered. "Mrs. White would like to take a goose like that back to Texas with her."

"All right," Faulk replied. "You catch the goose, and I'll get the shell."

Williams moved slowly toward the beautiful bird so as not to frighten it. The goose seemed to be almost tame, and he gazed calmly at the stranger moving toward him. However, just as Williams reached out to grab the goose, a pickup truck rattled down the road past the cemetery, and the noise startled the bird to flight.

At that very instant Faulk lifted the shell from Charles Whitehead's grave.

The goose circled slowly over the cemetery, flying low, and then flew due west toward Texas. The four men watched the great goose until it was out of sight.

Then they brushed some of the dirt from the shell, carefully wrapped it in paper, and went to deliver it to Mrs. White.

With the shell they brought the story of the blue goose, the unusual bird that had watched them take the shell from Charles Whitehead's grave and, after the shell had been removed, had flown westward.

"Do you suppose—No. No. It couldn't be—But I do wonder—," Mrs. White said, half to herself, when their story had ended.

She wondered more about the strange bird when she returned to Texas and heard a story from her niece, Mrs.

Eloise Ratcliff Adams, great-great-granddaughter of Missouri Loyless Whitehead.

Mrs. Adams lived in Glen Rose, Texas, at the time. On October 15, two days after the blue goose had circled Charles Whitehead's grave in Georgia and had flown westward, Mrs. Adams' thirteen-year-old daughter called to her from the yard.

"Mother! Come out quickly! There's a beautiful bird out here, a big one. Hurry!"

Mrs. Adams ran from the house and into the yard, and together she and her daughter watched a big blue goose, the first one either of them had ever seen, circle low over their house. Then it flew away—straight in the direction of Hemphill, Texas.

Mrs. White wondered about the bird as she took the conch to the cemetery at Hemphill and placed it on great-grandmother's grave.

"I know Charles wanted you to have the shell now," she said. "He sent it with his love."

There is a new conch affixed to Charles Whitehead's gravestone in Georgia, and the old shell at Missouri Whitehead's grave in Texas has a small marker reading, "To Missouri with Love from Charles."

The story of the conch is a treasured part of the Whitehead family tradition, and it is told and retold at family gatherings. Now the telling includes an account of a strange bird, a blue goose, that watched the removal of the shell from Charles Whitehead's grave and then flew halfway across the continent toward Missouri Whitehead's burial spot.

And they wonder, the people who tell the tale and the people who listen, if the bird took a message to Missouri Whitehead that her shell had been found and was being brought to her to sing for her an eternal song of remembrance.

CHARLES O. WHITEHEAD

1810   1853

There's a new shell affixed to Charles Whitehead's gravestone in Georgia.

The Curse Of Barnsley Gardens

"The scenery is beautiful, even more beautiful than you had described it to me, but, please, can't we build our house on another location?" Julia Barnsley asked her husband.

"Why?" Godfrey Barnsley replied. It had never occurred to him that Julia would object to the site he had chosen for what he intended to be the finest house in all of Georgia.

"Why?" he asked again. "What is wrong with this location? It's perfect, right here on top of this knoll with the spring and the creek at the rear. And sweeping down from the house will be our gardens stretching for acres and acres across the countryside. Why don't you like this site?" he asked again, still puzzled.

"Look," he continued, not waiting for her reply, "just let me show you what I have in mind. We'll build the center section with its three-story tower here, and then there'll be wings extending along the top of the knoll, about here, with—"

Julia interrupted him. "The plans for the house are perfect, but can't we put it somewhere else? Surely there is another suitable hill in the 10,000 acres of land you bought!

I keep remembering what the people in town said about this knoll having a curse on it. It frightens me."

"Nonsense!" Barnsley retorted sharply. "Surely you don't believe that foolish Indian superstition. I am surprised and disappointed in you, Julia!" To soften his words, for he seldom quarreled with his wife, Barnsley reached out and took her hand.

"This knoll is the one right location for our house, and I will build it here. We will call it Woodlands."

So Godfrey Barnsley, who had come from England some twenty years before and had become one of Georgia's wealthiest men, began that summer of 1844 to build the architectural showplace that was to bring tragedy to everyone who lived in it—just as the Cherokee Indian superstition warned.

Barnsley moved his wife and children from Savannah, the city where he had amassed his fortune but where he considered the climate unhealthy. They crowded into a small house they were to occupy while the mansion was being built.

It was rather like camping out, and the children delighted in the adventure, but Julia was uneasy. Her feeling of foreboding increased as she watched her husband direct the felling of the trees on the knoll and as she saw him show the workmen where to dig the foundations for Woodlands. She tried to be enthusiastic about the project, for she knew that Barnsley was building the house for her pleasure, but she kept hearing like a taunting echo, "There's a curse on the knoll—a curse—a curse—"

Barnsley was too busy planning and supervising the building of the grand mansion to be aware of his wife's increasing apprehension, and, after that first day at Woodlands when she had spilled out her fears to him, Julia never mentioned the topic again.

During the summer of 1845 Julia Barnsley became ill with what was diagnosed as a lung infection. Though she appeared for a while to be recovering, she died before the summer ended, and her infant son soon followed his mother in death. Thus Julia Scarborough Barnsley, age 34, and her baby were the first Barnsleys to fall victims to the "superstitious Indian curse."

The death of his beautiful young wife was a crushing sorrow to Godfrey Barnsley. For years, friends recall, he could not speak her name without weeping, and no woman ever replaced her in his love.

Soon after Julia's death, Barnsley took his children to New Orleans in a vain attempt to escape the memories of Julia that engulfed him so completely at Woodlands. After a time, when the acute grief had passed, Barnsley brought his family back to the north Georgia mountains. Work, he decided, would help him deal with his loneliness and grief, so he reassembled his workmen and ordered them to resume construction of Woodlands.

Barnsley devoted his entire attention to Woodlands. His money, his talents, his thoughts, and his strength were all directed toward one goal: Woodlands, the home and the gardens, must be a fitting memorial to his beloved Julia.

Progress was slow. Barnsley's requirement that every detail be perfect combined with the delay in receiving the marble mantels from Italy, the hand-fashioned paneling and the silver key plates from England, and the art treasures from throughout the world slowed the work.

A landscape architect, P. J. Berckman, came from Belgium to supervise the plantings of the formal gardens. The sweeping green lawns and terraces were centered with an oval maze of English boxwoods covering twenty acres, and along the divided drive and walkways were planted exotic trees: hemlocks and spruces from Norway, lindens, Japanese yews, firs, chestnuts, Scotch rowens. Grey boulders were hauled by ox team from the nearby mountains to provide the setting for the rock gardens.

As the gardens grew in beauty and scope, neighbors began referring to the place as Barnsley Gardens. In time the original name, Woodlands, was almost forgotten.

The house was not nearly finished in 1850 when Anna, the oldest daughter married T. C. Gilmour and moved to England. Work was still in progress in 1857 when the second daughter, Adelaide, married John K. Reid of New Orleans.

A year later when Adelaide came home to Woodlands to die, her father was still engrossed in the final phases of construction. Adelaide was buried beside her mother and her baby brother.

Once again Godfrey Barnsley had cause to recall the tale of the Indian curse.

The family had long ago moved from the small house or cabin where they first lived into a completed wing of the mansion. As various phases of construction were finished, the Barnsleys expanded the area of their living quarters.

It was soon after they moved into the big house that Barnsley confided to a friend, "Julia is here with me constantly. I see her walking in the garden, and her presence fills every room. Wherever I go at Woodlands, I feel her beside me."

When war came in 1861, the house was nearly completed. Only the handcarved stairway, which had been ordered from England, and the parquet floors remained to be installed.

Godfrey Barnsley was too old for military service, but his youngest sons, Lucian and George, joined the Confederate Army. A third son, Howard, the oldest, was in the Orient collecting plants and art treasures for Woodlands when the hostilities began. It was a mission from which he never returned. In 1862 Barnsley was notified that Howard had been killed by Chinese pirates.

Once again he wondered about the Indian curse.

It was in 1864 that Julia Barnsley, named for her mother, married Captain James P. Baltzelle, a provost marshall in the Confederate Army. Captain Baltzelle sent his bride to Savannah to refugee when Federal troops began moving toward Woodlands, and their daughter, Adelaide, was born in that port city.

The warning of the approach of the enemy was brought to Woodlands by Colonel Robert G. Earle, Second Alabama Cavalry. The Confederate officer rode through the formal gardens toward the house shouting,

"The Yankees are coming!"

A vanguard of the Federal troops was almost on his heels, and before Colonel Earle could escape he was shot from his saddle by a private from Company A, 98th Illinois Volunteers.

And so there was another grave at Woodlands, another reminder of the Indian curse.

The burial was delayed, however, while the Federal troops ransacked the house in search of the gold and treasure they expected to capture there. When they failed to find gold and when the treasures they had anticipated turned out to be paintings, statuary, and rare books, the soldiers vented their disgust by breaking the statuary, slashing the paintings, snatching the books from the shelves, smashing the china and crystal, and kicking holes in the woodwork.

Their most welcome prizes were found in the cellar where Godfrey Barnsley stored his Madeira wine, Scotch and brandies. The soldiers helped themselves.

Hours later Godfrey Barnsley stood on the front terrace and watched as the last of the invaders rode their horses through his rose garden and through his boxwood hedges. Then he turned and walked slowly into the ruins of his home, his Woodlands. "Julia—Julia," he sobbed in loneliness and frustration.

When he had recovered his composure and his strength, Barnsley made arrangements to bury his friend, Colonel Earle. The body was placed in a grave near the kitchen wing of the house, not far from where the soldier fell, and the spot was marked by a small stone from the hillside. Later the officer's name and his rank were carved on the stone.

Soon after the War ended, members of Colonel Earle's family came from Alabama to move his body home, but by that time the story of the curse on Barnsley Gardens had become so widespread that they could find no one willing to help them exhume the body. They had no choice but to leave the grave undisturbed and to return to Alabama.

The War left Godfrey Barnsley penniless. His mansion had been vandalized, his gardens were a tangle of weeds and vines, and the cotton business in which he had amassed his fortune was gone.

Even his sons did not return to Woodlands. Rather than take the oath of allegiance to the United States, the brothers sailed for South America. They settled in Sao Paulo, Brazil, where their descendants live until this day.

Barnsley left Woodlands, too. He moved to New Orleans where he had friends and where he intended to regain his lost fortune.

Into the shambles of Woodlands moved Julia and James Baltzelle and their little daughter, Adelaide. Baltzelle hoped to support his family by selling timber from the Barnsley lands, but it was an ill-fated venture. In 1868 he was helping cut timber for shipment by rail from Hall's Station when he was struck and killed by a falling tree.

The curse of Barnsley Gardens had claimed another victim.

After the death of her husband, Julia fled from Woodlands and took her child to New Orleans to live with Barnsley. It was in New Orleans that she met and married a German sea captain named Charles H. von Schwartz.

Von Schwartz probably saw the fabled Barnsley Gardens for the first time in 1873 when Julia brought her father's body home for burial.

As the group of mourners turned to leave the family burying ground, a neighbor observed, "Godfrey Barnsley is at peace now for the first time since his Julia died."

Nine-year-old Adelaide, or Addie as she was called, had accompanied her parents to the funeral. She looked at the massive house and the overgrown gardens, and she questioned and she wondered for no one had the patience or the perception to answer the questions that nagged at the mind of the child.

It would be years later, when she herself was mistress of Barnsley Gardens, that Addie would commune with the restless spirits of the dead and would understand the troubled feeling that crowded in upon her that day of her Grandfather Barnsley's funeral.

Addie was twenty-one when she came to Barnsley Gardens to stay. Her stepfather had died in 1885, and Addie and her mother, having nowhere else to go, came home to Barnsley Gardens.

As the two women hacked paths through the heavy undergrowth that had destroyed the symmetry of the gardens and as they worked together to make part of the old house livable, Julia talked with Addie about the grandeur of Woodlands as she remembered it from childhood. She told of the banquet table that seated forty guests, of Godfrey Barnsley's ingenious plan for providing running water in the bathrooms and kitchen by installing a cistern atop the tower in the center of the building, of the twenty-six-foot drawing room and the billiard room and the library with its leather-bound books.

131

Addie listened and tried to imagine how Barnsley Gardens looked in those years before the War. And when her mother wept over the departed glory, Addie comforted her by saying, "Don't cry, Mama. Just keep remembering how it used to be. We can restore it. I know we can."

Gradually, just as her grandfather had been obsessed with building Woodlands, Addie became obsessed with the determination to restore it.

Addie listened to other stories about Woodlands, too, stories that neighbors and former servants told about the Indian curse and about the tragedies that followed the building of Woodlands. She heard accounts of ghosts that roamed about the premises: her grandparents, Julia and Godfrey Barnsley, and the homesick spirit of Colonel Robert Earle.

She heard rumors, too, that her grandfather's body had been dug up by grave robbers who cut off his hand to use in pagan voodoo rites. Addie never repeated this rumor to her mother.

She never told her mother, either, when she herself began to see the ghosts at Barnsley Gardens. It was her grandmother, Julia Barnsley, whom Addie saw first, Julia walking among the scraggly boxwoods near the entrance of the house.

For as long as she lived at Barnsley Gardens, Addie continued to see her grandmother strolling around the grounds. She was aware, too, of the presence of a spirit, whom she recognized as Colonel Earle, wearing the grey uniform of the Confederacy.

Though she never saw him, Addie frequently heard in the late afternoon the scraping sound of her grandfather pushing his chair back from his desk in the library. The scraping of that chair had, years before, signaled the time for Godfrey Barnsley's pre-dinner toddy.

Addie heard, too, the laughter of the Barnsley children at play in a now-deserted wing of the house, and on some nights she was awakened by the noise of ghostly hammers wielded by invisible workmen trying to finish building Woodlands.

The presence of these ghosts served somehow to

133

strengthen Addie's determination to restore her ancestral home. Her dream of restoring Barnsley Gardens was shared by the man she married, A. A. Saylor, a chemist. But though they talked and planned and assured each other that Barnsley Gardens would be elegant again, they never had sufficient money to get the project underway.

And the Indian curse lingered at Barnsley Gardens.

Saylor died, leaving Addie to rear their young children alone. Then in 1906 a tornado swept down on Barnsley Gardens, destroying the roof and doing other damage. Mrs. Saylor, Addie, salvaged what furniture she could and moved her family into the undamaged wing of the house where she was to live until her death.

Despite these misfortunes, Addie Saylor never relinquished her dream of rebuilding Barnsley Gardens. From the time her sons, Preston and Harry, were babies, Addie talked with them of the former majesty of Barnsley Gardens and urged them to spend their lives bringing beauty and order back to their family home. The boys were intrigued by the stories Addie told, and they promised solemnly, as children will, to work together to make their mother's dream a reality.

But they forgot the curse, and they never reckoned that they would be the principals in Barnsley Gardens' greatest tragedy.

As they grew older, the brothers became suspicious and envious of each other. Preston, having an adventurous and daring nature, became a professional boxer and achieved some success in the ring. Harry, after service with the infantry in World War I, returned to Barnsley Gardens to live with his mother. Harry's return revived Addie's waning hopes of having the needed work done at Barnsley Gardens.

Preston's boxing career ended when he suffered serious head injuries in a fight. Those injuries, friends said, affected his mind to such an extent that it became necessary to have him committed to the state hospital for the insane.

Preston blamed Harry for having him confined, and he swore vengeance. In March, 1935, he escaped from the institution. Eight months later Preston appeared at Barnsley Gardens. He burst into the living room where Addie and Harry were talking (it was their favorite subject, the restoration of Barnsley Gardens that they were discussing), and he fired a single shot through Harry's heart.

Harry died in his mother's arms.

For seven more years Addie lived at Barnsley Gardens with her lost dreams. One son was dead, the other in prison. Now no one was left who loved Barnsley Gardens as she did or who wanted to make it beautiful again. Roofless walls crumbled, arches collapsed, trees grew through rotten flooring, vines crept through the broken windows.

In her lonely quarters, Addie Saylor watched the ghost of her grandmother stroll in the garden. She heard her grandfather scrape his chair across the floor in the library and heard the Barnsley children laugh and heard the pounding of phantom hammers. She met the restless spirit of Colonel Earle when she went to get water from the spring back of the house. They were, all of them, welcome, familiar companions.

Another apparition appeared. Harry's spirit came back to talk with his mother, to ask,

"Mama, is there really a curse on Barnsley Gardens? Is that why we've been plagued by tragedy? Is there really a curse here?"

And Addie remembered the story she had heard of a young woman named Julia Barnsley who begged her husband, "Please, can't we build our house on another location?"

Outracing The Devil

"The Devil is going to get you, Abram Simons," the preacher warned.

"You'd better quit your horse racing, and you'd better stop having dances at your tavern, and you'd better join the church. You're a sinful man, Abram Simons. The Devil is going to get you!"

Simons looked the preacher hard in the eye, but he did not reply, not right then. Instead he patted his horse's flank, took a firm hold of the reins, stepped into the stirrup, and swung easily into the saddle.

"The Devil will have to ride fast to catch me," he shouted back as he galloped down the road toward Washington, Georgia.

His horse's hoofs drowned out the final warning from the preacher: "You can't outrace the Devil, Abram Simons!"

The preacher's threats, the ones he heard, annoyed Captain Simons. It did not seem quite proper for a guest to be so critical of his host. When he recalled how readily the preacher, a circuit rider from the Carolinas, had accepted Mrs. Simons' invitation to dinner and how greedily he had

137

helped himself to the thick slices of roast beef and slabs of ham, Captain Simons became angry.

"The Devil, indeed!" he snorted as he urged his horse on.

The horse gained speed, and Captain Simons shifted his attention from the unpleasant episode with the visiting parson to the joy of riding a fast thoroughbred through the Georgia countryside. For not even threats of hellfire and damnation could long divert Captain Simons from his passion for breeding, training, and racing fine horses.

"Faster now! Come on, come on! Faster! You'll never win the race at this pace. Go—go—go!!" he urged his mount.

He hoped the three-year-old he was riding would win Washington's annual Washington Jockey Club race held the first Wednesday in March, only a few days away. Of all the horses Captain Simons had trained at his track near his tavern, this horse, Babylon, seemed most likely to win. Not only was Babylon fast, he also had style and pride, qualities which Captain Simons recognized and admired in horses and in human beings.

So as he rode toward Washington, where his main business consisted of hearing the political news of the week and of placing proper wagers on Babylon to win the race, he concentrated completely on the performance of his horse. Abram Simons (most people in the area called him Captain Simons in recognition of his participation in the Revolutionary War battle of Kettle Creek) lingered longer in Washington that he had intended. It was almost twilight when he unhitched Babylon from the poplar tree on the town's main street and headed home.

Because it was getting dark, Captain Simons rode slowly to protect Babylon from making a possible misstep. To have the horse become lame just before the big race would be a tragedy. Riding along in the deepening dusk, his mind went back to the events of the morning. It was not the first time that visiting ministers and even some of his pious neighbors had warned him about falling into the clutches of the Devil. Though he tried to push the thought aside, the idea of being chased and captured by the Devil nagged at him, making him uncomfortable.

Even Babylon's hoofbeats seemed to be tapping out in rhythm, "Devil's going to get you—Devil's going to get you—Devil's going to get you." And no matter how often he changed the pace or how hard he tried not to listen, the rhythmic message engulfed his consciousness.

He rode past Smyrna Church where, though he was not a member, he often accompanied his wife to services on meeting days. Just a little further along the familiar road he saw the lights of Simons' Tavern. The tavern was a big building, two stories tall, on a high hill, and when the lamps in the upstairs ballroom were lit their glow filtered through the trees and brightened the countryside.

Captain Simons welcomed the lights of home after his rather disturbing ride. He noticed, however, that flurries of sparks were rising from the stout chimneys at the ends of the tavern.

"I must order the servants again to be more careful about those fires," he said aloud. "The sparks could set the shingles on the roof afire, and the tavern would burn before we could haul enough water from the creek to put it out. Dangerous, those sparks are."

Thought of the creek brought a wry grin. His friends in Washington had teased him again about the creek. They had asked, half in jest, if he really did order his servants to pour water from the creek onto the red clay hill near his tavern so that the wheels of wagons would mire down and the drivers would have to come to his tavern for help and for refreshments.

He wondered how the story ever got started. It was not

139

such a bad idea, he mused, making a sticky mudhole on that steep hill. Seeing loaded wagons roll past his tavern without even a brief pause for food or drink did not pleasure him. But to have such a story spread abroad was not to the captain's liking.

He rode into the stable, gave instructions to the groom for the care of Babylon, and then went up the narrow back stairs to the second floor of the tavern. There his wife, Nancy, was standing in the doorway. Her hair, still dark and curly at middle age, was piled on top of her head and tied with a yellow velvet ribbon to match the yellow print in her full skirt.

"I was beginning to be worried about you," she said.

Strange, Captain Simons thought, that she should still worry about him after a quarter of a century of married life, but her concern pleased him. He started to tell her about the unpleasant predictions from the preacher and about how Babylon's hoofs seemed to be repeating, "Devil's going to get you—Devil's going to get you." But he decided against it. He did not wish to upset her.

In all their years together (they had been married in 1798) their only real disagreements had been on the subject of religion. Captain Simons, reared in the Jewish faith, would not join the Methodist Church—or any other—with his wife, and his failure to become a convert distressed her. However, he frequently accompanied her to Sunday services at Smyrna Church. On those occasions he and she rode in a carriage drawn by four perfectly matched white horses driven by a uniformed coachman.

Regular worshippers observed that when Captain Simons came with his wife to church—always a little late—the rustle of Mrs. Simons' fine silk skirts announced the couple's entrance into the sanctuary. The women whispered that the captain planned these late arrivals so that the entire

140

congregation could admire his wife and her elegant clothes. He was very proud of her.

So he did not mention his prophesied encounter with the Devil. Instead, after he had had supper, they went together into the ballroom where Mrs. Simons gave the servants directions about decorating the elaborate room for the ball the couple planned for members of the Washington Jockey Club and their guests.

Simons admired the wallpaper, as he always did when he entered the room. "Don't you like these hunting scenes better than you did those pictures of ladies dancing with scarves?" he asked his wife for at least the twelfth time. And for the twelfth time she agreed that she had liked the Grecian dancing scenes, considering them more suitable for the ballroom than the colorful hunt scenes her husband had selected.

The wallpaper for the dining room and the ballroom had been imported from England, but the ornate moldings in the two rooms had been fashioned on the place by local craftsmen. Captain Simons never failed to point out these decorative features to guests.

"Did you bring a newspaper from town?" Mrs. Simons asked her husband. "Would you like me to read the news to you?"

Captain Simons nodded and went to fetch the paper he had brought from Washington. Successful businessman—he had accumulated thousands and thousands of dollars—and civic leader that he was, he had never learned to read. He was a grown man before he could recognize the letters that formed his own name, but ever since he could remember he had been able to do sums and calculate figures rapidly in his head.

This mastery of mental arithmetic was largely responsible for the captain's business success. It seemed that every venture in which he became involved added gold to his holdings. He enjoyed making money, and spending it on his beloved wife gave him added pleasure.

"The money is yours—do whatever you want with it," he would tell her. "Making it is more fun than spending it."

Years later, after Captain Simons' death and after his rich widow had married the Rev. Jesse Mercer, people recalled how generous Captain Simons had been with her. They reckoned he would not have objected when she used her inheritance to help found a Baptist college. That is what happened: Mrs. Nancy Mills Simons Mercer gave about $400,000 to help found and endow Mercer University.

During their married life, Captain Simons depended heavily on his wife to keep him informed about news of importance. If he was in Washington when the rider arrived with the mail, he always stood on the edge of the crowd and listened closely as the postmaster read aloud the major news items from the Savannah paper. Later Nancy would read the paper to him, column by column, when he brought a copy home.

That night, however, he could not concentrate on the news. He kept hearing, "The Devil's going to get you—the Devil's going to get you—the Devil's going to get you!"

Perhaps that is the night Captain Simons began preparing for his funeral. Nobody, of course, knows for sure, but it was about this time, friends recalled, that Captain Simons selected his burial place.

His wife had assumed that he would be buried in the cemetery at Smyrna Church, even though he was not a member there, but the captain had other ideas.

"I don't want to be crowded into a graveyard with strangers," he declared.

The spot he selected for his grave was a wooded knoll a short distance behind his tavern. The knoll afforded a clear view of the comings and goings at the tavern and of his race track. It was an ideal spot, he concluded.

"The spot he selected for his grave was a wooded knoll a short distance behind his tavern."

—"the wall with its iron gate still protects his lonely burial place."

Once he had chosen the site, Captain Simons supervised the building of a stone wall, shoulder high, with a plain iron gate to enclose his future burial ground. Some of his associates thought Captain Simons' preparations for death a bit strange though they did agree that his choice of a grave site was fitting for a man of his interests.

Choosing the site and building the wall did not complete Captain Simons' personalized funeral plans, however. The entire countryside was shocked when the captain announced,

"I want to be buried standing up with my musket at my side so I can shoot the Devil." And he was quite serious.

No suggestions or reasoning could change his mind, so when Captain Abram Simons died about 1824, he was stood to rest inside the walled enclosure near his tavern and his racetrack, and his musket was placed at his side. He was ready for any possible encounter with his adversary, the Devil.

That should be the end of the story of Captain Abram Simons, but it is not.

Only a few scattered bricks mark the place where his tavern once stood, the once-busy trade route is seldom used now, and his racetrack is lost in a dense forest, but the wall with its iron gate still protects his lonely burial place.

Some residents of the area say that on certain nights they hear distinctly the sound of horse's hoofs galloping down the deserted road near Captain Abram Simons' tavern. There is never a horse and rider—just the clatter of hoofs.

And some folks who hear the invisible horse say it is the ghost of Captain Simons out exercising one of his fine steeds. Other folks say that, listening carefully, they hear the hoofs pounding out, "Devil's going to get you—Devil's going to get you—Devil's going to get you." They know on those nights that Captain Abram Simons' ghost, riding on Babylon, is trying to outrun the Devil.

They hear distinctly the sound of horse's hoofs galloping down the deserted road near Captain Abram Simons' tavern.

The Chanting Friars

It was a hot July night in the early 1930s when Mrs. Courtney Thorpe first heard the ghostly chanting of the Franciscan friars and the Gaule Indians.

The weather was too muggy for her to be comfortable inside the house, so Mrs. Thorpe walked out onto the front porch where she plumped up a pillow in a rocking chair and sat down. She hoped a sea breeze would spring up before bedtime, as it often did, but there was no promise of one. The leaves on the giant oaks hung motionless, and the marsh grasses stretching along the South Newport River did not stir. Even the garlands of grey Spanish moss were still.

The mosquitoes stirred, though. As soon as she sat down, Mrs. Thorpe heard the annoying insects buzzing around her, and she felt one bite her on the ankle.

"You can't get comfortable anywhere on a night like this," Mrs. Thorpe complained as she rose from her chair to get the squirt gun with its mosquito spray.

"Quick, Henry, the Flit!" she said, repeating the words of a popular commercial. "Unfortunately, there's no Henry to get the Flit, so I'll have to wield the spray gun myself. I do

147

hope Essie filled it before she left this afternoon—I can never pour the liquid in without spilling it," she added.

The sprayer felt reassuringly heavy when she lifted it from the shelf near the front door. Pumping the handle vigorously, Mrs. Thorpe directed a thick mist of the insect repellent around her rocking chair. Then she sat down and pointed the nozzle toward her feet, spraying them until her stockings felt damp.

"There. That should keep the pests away for awhile!" She put the sprayer down beside her chair, in easy reach if she should need to use it again.

She rocked slowly and fanned herself with the newspaper she had brought out with her. Some nights she read on the porch, but tonight the added heat from the electric bulb would have been unbearable. The light would attract other insects, too, she decided, so she rocked and fanned in the dark.

Mrs. Thorpe did not feel the late breeze when it began blowing in from the Atlantic across St. Catherines Island and the marshes and the river. She had dozed in her chair, and when she awakened—it must have been around midnight—she was chilly and stiff, and mosquitoes were feasting on her ankles.

She brushed the offenders away. Then as she rose to go into the house, Mrs. Thorpe heard music from across the marshes. It was singing she heard, a chorus of men's voices, but it was strange and unfamiliar. The singers were chanting with one strong voice calling out a phrase and the chorus echoing his words over and over again. She could not make out the words though the voices were distinct, not loud but distinct.

Mrs. Thorpe stood on her porch listening to the singing for five full minutes before the voices faded away, leaving only the familiar night sounds, the sighing of the marsh grasses, the dull hum of insects, the rustling of leaves, the serenade of a mocking bird.

The breeze had made the night pleasant, but Mrs. Thorpe could not sleep. She could not free her mind of the recollection of the chanting she had heard, and it disturbed her that she could not identify the music or tell where it came from.

There were no close neighbors (her father-in-law's home just south of hers on the river bluff was the only house within miles), so she knew the music could not have come from a radio or a record player. And it did not sound like anything she had ever heard on radio or record. Mrs. Thorpe loved music, and she had quite a collection of classical and religious records, including recordings of folk songs and spirituals from the Georgia sea islands. Nothing in her collection sounded like the singing she had heard.

Yet with all its strangeness there was something elusively familiar about the music. It sounded like—like—. She could not decide. There was a religious quality about the rhythm, she recalled, something that made her think of church. Church! That was it! The chanting reminded her of parts of the service at the Cathedral of St. John the Baptist in Savannah where she went occasionally with friends, and somehow it brought to mind also the annual blessing of the shrimp fleet at Darien.

So it had to be Catholic oriented. Catholic? There had not been many Catholics—certainly not enough to form a choir—along that part of the coast since the Spanish missionaries converted the Guale Indians to Catholicism back in the 1570s, she reminded herself.

It was almost dawn before Mrs. Thorpe finally went to sleep, and before sleep came she had almost convinced herself that she had heard the antiphonal chants from a Catholic worship service. Her dreams were peopled with Guale Indians

149

and brown-robed Franciscan friars.

A few nights later her experience was repeated. She heard again, blown by the wind from St. Catherines Island, the chanted call and response of Catholic worship. Yet she could not quite believe that she was hearing ghostly music coming almost four hundred years from the past.

Mrs. Thorpe was not a native of the Georgia coast, and though she had lived on the South Newport River at the plantation called Lebanon for many years, she was not familiar with all the local legends. So on her next trip to Darien she asked some discrete questions.

"Has anyone," she asked a friend whom she met in the grocery store, "ever seen the ghosts of the Franciscan friars whom the Indians murdered?"

Her friend laughed, the way people do who discredit the possibility of the existence of ghosts, and replied, "Oh, there have been reports of people seeing the ghosts of Catholic missionaries on some of the islands. They were supposed to be the ghosts of the murdered friars. But, of course, nobody took the stories seriously. At least I didn't!" And she laughed again.

So Mrs. Thorpe did not mention the eerie music she had heard. Instead she went to the library to refresh her knowledge of the early efforts of the Spanish to Christianize the Indians.

She read about Pedro Menéndez de Avilés, Spanish governor of St. Augustine, who stopped at St. Catherines Island while sailing up the Georgia coast in 1566. She read, too, the account of how the Indians credited the cross that Menéndez set up on the island with bringing a drought-breaking rain and expressed their gratitude by welcoming the missionaries he sent to civilize them and to convert them to Christianity.

She read about the Franciscan friars who came in the late

1570s to establish missions and who for more than a century taught, baptized, doctored, comforted, and disciplined the Indians. One sentence in the account of the establishment of the Spanish missions was of great interest to Mrs. Thorpe:

"The friars taught the Indians the rudiments of church ritual and antiphonal chants."

Antiphonal chants—that is what she had heard! Mrs. Thorpe was positive that her late night concerts were the chants of the Guale Indians and their Catholic missionary teachers.

After she had heard the chanting on four or five nights, Mrs. Thorpe told some of her close friends (not the one in the grocery store) about her experiences, and she invited them to come out to Lebanon to listen. But on the nights that the friends came to sit with her on the wide front porch, there was never any music. Though they concentrated and listened intently, all they ever heard were the usual night sounds: insects humming, a mocking bird singing, wind moving through the trees and marshes.

The silences embarrassed Mrs. Thorpe for she knew her friends must think she made up the entire story, or worse still, that she was a bit mentally unbalanced. The friends were polite and sympathetic, and not one of them hinted that Mrs. Thorpe might possess an over-active imagination. The truth is, the visitors were disappointed: they really wanted to hear the peculiar chanting Mrs. Thorpe had described.

On the nights when she was alone, not all of them but many, Mrs. Thorpe continued to hear the chanting. Her enjoyment of the music deepened as she became more familiar with the stylized call and response, and as the weeks passed she almost felt that she knew the men who were participating in the ritual.

"Is that Father Pedro de Corpa leading the chants tonight, or is it that saintly giant, Father Velascola?" she would ask

151

herself.

She continued to regret that her friends had never heard the chanting. Somehow she felt selfish having it all to herself. Then one day it occurred to her that she might record the ceremonial chants and then play the recordings for people who were interested.

She got her recording equipment ready (this was before the time of tape and transistors). She bought blank records on which she hoped to capture the chanting, and she made sure that her extension cord was in good repair and that it would reach easily from the electrical plug in the hall to the shelf on the porch where she planned to put the recording machine.

To be certain that everything was working as it should she made a test recording of herself telling the background of the hearing of the phantom voices and another recording of Essie, her maid, singing as she worked among the flowers in the yard. The equipment worked perfectly.

The next few nights were stormy with blowing rain making it impossible for her to take her recording equipment out onto the porch. She waited impatiently for the weather to become clear and calm for it was only on clear and calm nights that she had heard the chanting.

When such a night finally arrived, Mrs. Thorpe checked her recording equipment again before she put it on the porch shelf. Satisfied that there were no problems, she settled herself in her favorite rocker and waited.

The mosquitoes were annoying, just as they had been that first night she heard the phantom voices, and, just as she had done that night, Mrs. Thorpe combatted them by spraying insect repellent around her chair and on her legs. This night, however, she did not go to sleep but remained wide awake and alert.

It was late, near midnight, and Mrs. Thorpe was about to

From across the marshes at Lebanon came the music of the chanting friars.

give up her patient, silent vigil when she heard the voices. The sound came from across the marshes, low and blurred at first as though the singers were weary or were uncertain of their musical parts. Then the volume of the chanting increased and the words became so distinct that Mrs. Thorpe could hear each one clearly.

She quickly turned on the recording machine.

"Don't stop singing! Please don't stop the chants!" she prayed silently to the unseen chorus.

Assured that the machine was operating properly, Mrs. Thorpe returned to her chair to listen to the strange nocturnal concert. Never before had the chanting been so stirring, so personal. It almost seemed that the singers were calling to her, were inviting her to come across the marshes and across the years and join them in worship and praise.

Suddenly she smelled smoke.

153

The recorder was afire.

Mrs. Thorpe hurried into the hall and yanked the electrical plug from the outlet with one hand while she snatched up a small rug with the other. She threw the rug over the blazing recorder and smothered the flames.

It had lasted only a few seconds, but the fire had completely consumed the machine and the record it had been making.

Now the chanting grew very loud, rising to a crescendo of exuberance. Then there was silence, sudden and absolute.

Mrs. Thorpe never heard the chanting of the friars and their Indian converts again.

Next morning she called an electrician to the house to check the wiring and the charred remains of her recording machine. That man could find nothing wrong, nothing to explain the cause of the destructive fire.

"No, ma'am," he said to her, "I sure don't know what caused the fire. It didn't start from an electrical or a mechanical defect. I don't know what could have happened. It's strange."

Mrs. Thorpe did not try to explain to him that she had been trying to record four-hundred-year-old antiphonal chants sung by Spanish missionaries and Guale Indians.

She did try to explain the disastrous recording session to her friends. They kept insisting that she had never really heard friars and Indians singing, that the music brought to her by the sea winds came from across the marshes where a revival meeting was in progress. They reminded her that often in rural churches a song leader sings a line of a hymn and the congregation repeats it.

"But," Mrs. Thorpe, who knew what she had heard, countered, "I distinctly heard the words and phrases from the Roman Catholic liturgy.

"How many rural Georgia Baptist choirs sing in Latin?"

NOTE

This page in this book, as well as the following pages, is reserved for Jeffrey's photograph. Jeffrey's photograph appears 13 times on this page and on each of the following pages. Readers with normal vision should not look too long, however.